MW00789790

Enjoying Christ as the Word and the Spirit through Prayer

WITNESS LEE

Living Stream Ministry
Anaheim, California

© 2002 Living Stream Ministry

All rights reserved. No part of this work may be reproduced or transmitted in any form or by any means—graphic, electronic, or mechanical, including photocopying, recording, or information storage and retrieval systems—without written permission from the publisher.

First Edition, September 2002.

ISBN 978-0-7363-1983-6

Published by

Living Stream Ministry
2431 W. La Palma Ave., Anaheim, CA 92801 U.S.A.
P. O. Box 2121, Anaheim, CA 92814 U.S.A.

Printed in the United States of America

08 09 10 11 12 13 / 9 8 7 6 5 4 3 2

CONTENTS

PREFACE

This book is composed of messages given by Brother Witness Lee in Los Angeles, California in the summer training of 1965. The subject of the summer training was the inner life and the church life. Chapter seven of this book has already been published in *The Enjoyment of Christ,* which was spoken concurrently with the messages in this book.

CHAPTER ONE

TRANSFERRING THE WORD
INTO THE SPIRIT BY PRAYER

Scripture Reading: John 1:1, 14; 6:63; 1 Cor. 15:45b; Acts 6:4; 2:42; 10:9; Isa. 56:7

The Bible reveals that God is our enjoyment and that all the riches of God, what God is in His fullness, are the riches of Christ (Eph. 3:8, 19b). All the fullness of God is embodied in Christ (Col. 1:19) and becomes the items of the riches of Christ. The reality of Christ is the Spirit, who is the Spirit of reality (John 14:17), and all that Christ is, that is, all the riches of Christ, are revealed in the Word (1:1). Therefore, in order to know the riches of Christ, we have to know the Word, which is the revelation of all that Christ is. Moreover, the place in which we realize the Triune God is our human spirit (3:6). In order to realize Christ and always enjoy Him, we have to exercise our spirit. There is no other way to enjoy Him, and there is no other organ with which we can enjoy Him. We have to exercise our spirit to realize all that God is in Christ through the Holy Spirit and as revealed in the Word. These five items—God, Christ, the Holy Spirit, the Word, and our spirit—are the factors of our enjoyment of God.

CHRIST FIRST BEING THE WORD
AND THEN BECOMING THE SPIRIT

Christ is first revealed as the Word, and in His resurrection He was transferred from the Word into the Spirit. Therefore, our experience of Christ is an experience of constantly transferring the word into the Spirit. John 6:63 is a great verse in the Bible. It says, "It is the Spirit who gives life; the flesh profits nothing; the words which I have spoken to you are spirit and are life." The word is spirit, and the Spirit is life. The word is life to us only when it is transferred into the Spirit. We do not have the word of life directly. We need a step in between; that is, the word must be spirit in order to be life to us. Without this step, the word is mere knowledge to us. In order to know the Scriptures and to know life, we must be familiar with and very clear about all these principles. Then we will have the keys to open the Word. Otherwise, no matter how many times we read the Word, we will read it in a blind and foolish way, and it will never be clear to us.

The four Gospels tell us that the Lord Jesus came as the Word. In the beginning, in eternity before the foundation of the world, He was the Word, and in time He came in incarnation (John 1:1, 14). Therefore, the New Testament begins with Christ as the Word. Then at the end of the Gospel of John Christ became the Spirit as the breath of life (20:22). This Gospel begins with the Word and ends with the Spirit. The Word and the Spirit are not two persons; they are one person with two aspects. First He was the Word, and eventually He became the Spirit. With the help of the Epistles we can realize who this Spirit is. The proper term used for this Spirit is the "life-giving Spirit." First Corinthians 15:45b says, "The last Adam became a life-giving Spirit." Again we see that the Bible is opened by this one principle, that the Word becomes the Spirit as life. Christ is the Word, Christ has become the Spirit, and this Spirit is the life-giving Spirit.

THE WAY TO TAKE THE WORD AS LIFE

It is by the Word through the Spirit that Christ is life to us and imparts life to us. According to the letter of the Bible, many Christians know that Christ is life, but not many can say how Christ can be life to us practically. We must be clear that Christ is life to us because He is the Word who became the Spirit who gives life. Now in order to receive, realize, and experience Christ as our life, we must know the Word and how to transfer the Word into the life-giving Spirit. This is the way to take Christ as life.

From my youth I heard Christian teachers say that the word of the Bible is life. However, they did not tell me how the black and white printed words of the Bible can be life. The answer is that the word in black and white must be transferred into the Spirit. If the word is merely in letters, it is not life; it is mere knowledge that kills (2 Cor. 3:6). It is when the word is transferred into the Spirit that it becomes life, because it is not the words directly but the Spirit who gives life.

THE DISCIPLES "READING" CHRIST AS THE LIVING WORD IN THE GOSPELS

In the four Gospels the disciples received the Word, but they did not yet receive the Spirit. It is after the four Gospels, in the Acts and the Epistles, that they received the Spirit. This means that the Word which the disciples received in the four Gospels was transferred into the Spirit, whom they experienced and contacted in the Acts and the Epistles. By this time the disciples dealt not only with the Word but also with the Spirit.

At the time of the Gospels the disciples did not have the New Testament. However, they still had and dealt with Christ as the Word. First John 1:1 says, "That which was from the beginning, which we have heard, which we have seen with our eyes, which we beheld and our hands handled, concerning the Word of life." At that time, what Peter, John, and all the disciples heard, saw, handled, and dealt with was the Word. In his first Epistle, John did not say that they had seen the Son of God or Jesus Christ. Rather, they saw, heard, looked upon, and even handled the Word. This Word was not a composition written in black and white letters. This Word was a living Person, whom the disciples "read" day by day. This Person is the Triune God who was incarnated to be a man by the name of Jesus. This Jesus had many "stories" for the disciples to read. John 1:14 says, "And the Word became flesh and tabernacled among us (and we beheld His glory, glory as of the only Begotten from the Father), full of grace and reality." Peter, James, John, and all the early disciples beheld the glory of this living Person, and in this way they "read" Him.

From the time Peter, Andrew, James, and John were called, they started to "read" this living Person. Wherever

they went with this Person, they beheld this Person and what
He was doing. In this way they "read" Him for three and a
half years. Once on the sea they experienced a violent storm.
They were frightened by that storm, but this living Person as
the living Word lay there still asleep (Matt. 8:24-25). When
He awakened, He simply gave the order to the air and the
water for the storm to stop (v. 26). Then the disciples mar-
veled, saying, "What kind of man is this that even the winds
and the sea obey Him?" (v. 27). What they were doing at that
time was reading the living Word.

Later, Peter, James, and John went to the mountain with
the living Word, where they beheld Him further. All of a
sudden His face was shining like the sun. Peter said, "Lord, it
is good for us to be here; if You are willing, I will make three
tents here, one for You and one for Moses and one for Elijah"
(17:4). Peter did not read the living Word clearly, so he began
to speak foolishly. Then a voice from heaven said, "This is My
Son, the Beloved, in whom I have found My delight. Hear
Him!" (v. 5). Moses and Elijah disappeared from view, leaving
Jesus Himself alone. This was the way Peter read the living
Word.

When they came down from the mountain, those who took
up the temple tax came to Peter and asked him whether or
not Jesus paid the tax. Peter replied, saying yes (vv. 24-25).
When he came into the house, Jesus asked Peter, "From
whom do the kings of the earth receive custom or poll tax,
from their sons or from strangers?" It is as if Jesus said, "Do
the kings on the earth collect tax from their own son? Did you
not hear on the mountain that I am the Son of God? Why then
did you tell the tax collectors that I, the Son of the King, have
to pay the tax?" When Peter was corrected by the Lord, he
may have wanted to say, "Then I am wrong. You should not
pay the temple tax." However, Jesus agreed to pay the tax, but
not in a way that was easy for Peter. Peter had to do something difficult. The Lord said, "But that we do not stumble
them, go to the sea and cast a hook, and take the first fish
that comes up. And when you open its mouth, you will find a
stater; take that and give it to them for Me and you" (v. 27).
Peter must have been very troubled. While he was throwing

the hook into the sea, he may have said to himself, "I do not know from what direction the fish will come, and it must be a fish with a coin in its mouth. I simply cannot believe this. I have to learn the lesson. From now on I should not say anything. I should keep my mouth shut and not get involved." It must have been the Lord's intention at that time to educate the foolish Peter not to say anything when the tax gatherer came. He simply should have said, "Please wait. Let me go ask Jesus. I do not know anything, and I have no ground or right to say anything. Let the Master speak." In this way Peter read much of the living Word.

According to the four Gospels, Peter may have read the Lord Jesus more than anyone else. After the Lord's resurrection, when the day of Pentecost came, Peter stood up to speak. After being educated by the Lord, Peter did much talking, not in nonsense but in the Spirit and in life. We all must learn the way to read the Word. We should drop the traditional way of reading. The old way does not give any revelation; it gives only dead knowledge in black and white letters.

THE GOSPELS BEING WRITTEN ACCORDING TO
WHAT THE DISCIPLES "READ" OF THE LIVING WORD

The four Gospels were written by the early disciples based on what they had read of Christ as the living Word. First they read something of the Lord, and then they put what they had read into writing for us to read. Before John wrote chapters fourteen through seventeen of his Gospel, he "read" the Word by hearing the Lord. Some of what the disciples read of the Lord was His spoken words, but some of what they read were the living, walk, and acts of the Lord Jesus. They saw how Jesus acted, behaved, and dealt with people. Then after they saw all these things, they put them into writing for us to read. They were the first ones who received the Word; we are the next generation of those who receive it.

THE LIVING WORD BECOMING THE SPIRIT
IN THE ACTS AND THE EPISTLES

The four Gospels reveal Christ as the living Word, whom the disciples read day by day for three and a half years. At that time the Lord Jesus was the Word, but He was not the Spirit. In the Acts and the Epistles, however, the Lord Jesus was no longer only the Word to the disciples. By that time the disciples were dealing with Christ as the life-giving Spirit (1 Cor. 15:45b). It was through crucifixion and resurrection that this Jesus, who is the Word, was transferred into the Spirit.

THE PRACTICAL WAY TO TRANSFER
THE WORD INTO THE SPIRIT

In our own experience, however, we need to see how we can practically enjoy Christ as the Word transferred into the Spirit. It is hard to say whether today we are dealing with and enjoying the Lord as the Word or as the Spirit. If we simply study the word in the way taught by seminaries, for example, we will enjoy the Lord mainly as knowledge in the mind, although by His mercy we may unconsciously enjoy Him a little as the Spirit. Today, however, we are enjoying the Lord as the Word more in our spirit than in our mind. Eventually we will enjoy Him entirely as the Spirit in our spirit. All that we know of Him as the Word must be transferred into the Spirit. Then eventually we will enjoy the Lord not only as the Word but also as the life-giving Spirit.

The way to transfer Christ as the Word into the Spirit is to open our heart, open our spirit, and exercise our spirit to pray. In the four Gospels there is the Word who was "read" by the early disciples, and in the Acts there is the Spirit. Between the record of the four Gospels and the first part of Acts, the disciples prayed for ten days. It was by prayer that the Word was transferred into the Spirit. From that time on Peter became a praying person. This is why in chapter six Peter said, "We will continue steadfastly in prayer and in the ministry of the word" (v. 4). Prayer comes first, then the ministry of the word. To "continue steadfastly in prayer" means that their prayer never ceased. Acts 2:42 confirms that all the disciples continued steadfastly in prayer.

In Acts 10 Cornelius sent his servants to call Peter. At that time what was Peter doing? He was on the housetop praying (v. 9). In the four Gospels we see a talking Peter, not a praying Peter. Today too many of the brothers are talking brothers.

Sometimes they talk about the messages, but sometimes they just gossip. There is not much praying. In Acts, however, the talking Peter became a praying person. The disciples had already read Christ as the Word in the four Gospels. They already knew the Word clearly. Now what they needed was to transfer the Word into the Spirit by praying.

Consider what the one hundred and twenty disciples prayed for during those ten days before Pentecost. Someone may think that Peter prayed for his wife, that John and James prayed for their father's fishing business; that Andrew prayed for his home in Galilee, and that Mary and Martha prayed for Lazarus. However, this is not so. The Lord Jesus had told them to wait for the promise of the Father. He said, "But you shall receive power when the Holy Spirit comes upon you, and you shall be My witnesses both in Jerusalem and in all Judea and Samaria and unto the uttermost part of the earth" (1:8). In verse 22 Peter said concerning the selection of Matthias, "One of these should become a witness of His resurrection with us." They needed to select one to make up the number twelve, so they could adequately bear witness of Jesus. The disciples must have realized that for them to be the Lord's witnesses required that Christ be wrought into them.

By these two passages we can realize what the disciples must have been praying during those ten days. They must have said, "Lord, we have given up everything other than You. We were Galileans, but we have given up our home and our country. Now we are here simply as empty vessels. This little upper room is just like an altar, and we are lying on the altar waiting to be filled by You, possessed by You, taken over by You, and mingled with You. Lord, we have been reading all that You are for three and a half years. Now You have gone to the heavens, but You told us we must be Your witnesses on the earth. How can we do this? Lord, we are here open to You. Come to fill us. Come to take us over. Come to possess us, occupy us, and saturate us."

The disciples did not pray in a superficial way. Their prayer must have been a deep one. The one hundred and twenty had given up their homes, their relatives, their jobs, their goals, their fame, and their everything. The Lord had told them that they would be His witnesses, but they could not be His witnesses without being filled with Him. They needed the Lord to take them over and possess, occupy, fill, saturate, empower, and equip them. This must have been the content of their prayer. It was by this prayer, praying what they had been reading of Christ as the Word, that what they read was transferred into the Spirit. Therefore, from the day of Pentecost they were truly one with the Lord in spirit, and the Lord was one with them.

This is why when Saul of Tarsus persecuted Stephen and the other disciples, the Lord Jesus said to him, "Saul, Saul, why are you persecuting Me?" (9:4). When Saul asked, "Who are You, Lord?," the Lord answered, "I am Jesus, whom you persecute." (v. 5). Saul may have thought, "I persecuted Peter, James, John, and Stephen, but I never persecuted Jesus." However, by speaking to Saul in this way, the Lord revealed that to persecute His disciples was to persecute Him. Jesus was one with Peter, John, James, and all the disciples, because He was not only the Word but also the Spirit. From the day of Pentecost, the Word had been transferred into the Spirit. From that day the early disciples dealt not only with the Lord as the Word but also with Christ as the Spirit.

OUR NEED ALWAYS TO PRAY
WITH THE WORD THAT WE HAVE HEARD

The principle here is that whenever we read, hear, or know something of the Lord, we have to pray. We must keep this principle not only as individuals but also in our corporate life. The proper way to have a message meeting is that after the message we leave time for all the brothers and sisters to pray together. We should not simply give them a message and close the meeting. We have to pray to transfer the Word we hear into the Spirit. In the Spring of 1961 I was with the young people in Manila. During all those days, they spent more time praying than listening to the messages. For about two weeks, morning and night, those young people prayed. They prayed before coming to the meeting, and they prayed in the meeting. There was no real start to the meetings. Everyone simply prayed when they came. The prayer lasted for a long time, sometimes almost an hour before the message began. The message was finished in thirty or forty minutes, and then they prayed for about another hour. There were about one hundred young people, and all of them prayed, sometimes fifty or sixty in each meeting. That was a real move of the Lord in Manila that prepared them for some persecution that was to come. The prayer in that conference strengthened the whole church there. It also laid a good foundation for the church in Manila so that even today two-thirds of the members in the church are young people.

I do not mean that we should change the form of our meetings. Rather, we need to change our attitude, realization, and way of life. In the poor situation today, many people do not pray. They merely "come to church" at 11:00 A.M. on the Lord's Day to sit and listen to a message. We have to turn this situation around. We must be revolutionary to have a new kind of situation. The brothers and the sisters must be helped to learn how to pray and to have a prayer life. Then when they come to the meeting, they will come to pray. Isaiah 56:7 says, "My house will be called a house of prayer for all the peoples." All the brothers and sisters should come to the meeting to pray. We should not have too much singing; rather, we need more prayer to dig our heart, prepare our heart, and open our spirit. Then we can have a time for the ministry of the word, and when we speak the word, it will be living and will strike the spirit of the hearers. After the word is given, we still should have an additional time for prayer.

We should allow all of the attendants in the meeting to pray. At certain times in Taipei, there was not enough time for everyone to pray one by one, so the brothers and sisters began to pray at the same time, two or three thousand people all opening their mouths to pray. It was not that we encouraged them to do this; they did it spontaneously because everyone wanted to pray. At the beginning of 1961 we had a conference on the building of God. This conference was wonderful simply due to the fact that all the attendants spent much time in prayer. We must transfer the Word into the Spirit by our prayer.

In the four Gospels the early disciples had the Word for three and a half years, but they did not yet have the Spirit. At that time Christ was only the Word to them. It was through their prayer for ten days that Christ was transferred to them in their experience as the Spirit. From that time on they became a praying people, dealing not only with the Word but also with Christ as the life-giving Spirit. We all must keep the principle of transferring the word we have heard into the Spirit by our prayer.

CHAPTER TWO

SERVING THE LORD WITH PRAYER MORE THAN WITH THE OUTWARD WORD

Scripture Reading: Col. 3:16-17; Eph. 5:18-19; 1 Thes. 5:16-20; Eph. 6:17-18; Heb. 10:19-22; 4:16; John 6:63

In the four Gospels the Lord Jesus came as the Word. Then through His crucifixion and resurrection He was transfigured into the Spirit (1 Cor. 15:45b). After His resurrection and ascension, from the book of Acts through all the Epistles, the Lord Jesus is the life-giving Spirit. Therefore, in our experience we need to learn how to transfer the Lord as the Word into the Spirit. We need to know the Lord as the Word, the expression, the revelation, the manifestation, of God, but we need more than this. After we know Him as the Word, we need Him to be transferred into the Spirit that we may not only know Him but also experience Him.

In the four Gospels the Lord Jesus is revealed as the Word, the expression, the manifestation, of God for us to know. At that time Jesus was always among the early disciples for them to see, to study, and to know. Day by day throughout those three and a half years, Peter and the other disciples knew the Lord more and more. However, when we come to the book of Acts and the Epistles, we see the Lord Jesus as the life-giving Spirit indwelling our spirit (Rom. 8:16; 2 Tim. 4:22), not mainly for us to know but to partake of, taste, enjoy, and experience. Here we have two steps in our dealing with the Lord. The first step is to know Him as the Word, the more the better. The second step is to enjoy Him, to taste Him, and to experience Him—the more deeply the better. The principle is that we all must learn how to transfer the Lord as the Word into the Spirit.

BEING FILLED WITH THE WORD
THAT HAS BEEN TRANSFERRED INTO THE SPIRIT

Colossians 3:16 and 17 say, "Let the word of Christ dwell in you richly in all wisdom, teaching and admonishing one another with psalms and hymns and spiritual songs, singing with grace in your hearts to God. And whatever you do in word or in deed, do all things in the name of the Lord Jesus, giving thanks to God the Father through Him." These two verses show us that psalms, hymns, and spiritual songs come out of the word that fills us. When we are filled with the word, we give praises and thanks with psalms, hymns, and songs. The parallel passage in Ephesians 5:18 and 19 says, "And do not be drunk with wine, in which is dissoluteness, but be filled in spirit, speaking to one another in psalms and hymns and spiritual songs, singing and psalming with your heart to the Lord." Of the two passages in these sister books, one tells us that when we are filled with the word, we praise the Lord with psalms, hymns, and songs, while the other says that when we are filled in spirit, we praise with psalms, hymns, and songs. This proves that the word becomes the Spirit to us. When we are filled with the word in a proper way, we are at the same time filled in spirit.

By our own experience we know that the word must become the Spirit. Otherwise, we can never praise adequately. To praise with hymns is not something merely from the mind; our praising must be from the spirit. When our spirit is touched by the word as the Spirit, we have praise within us.

When the word spoken to us comes into us, it becomes the Spirit. Then when we speak it to others, it becomes the word again, and when they receive it, it becomes the Spirit to them. The Spirit going out becomes the word, and the word received in a proper way becomes the Spirit. If the word does not become the Spirit, it is mere knowledge, the letter that kills (2 Cor. 3:6). If we receive the word only in our mind, it is knowledge in letter, but when we receive the word into our spirit, it becomes Spirit. Moreover, when the word becomes Spirit, it becomes life.

PRAYER BEING THE UNIQUE WAY
TO RECEIVE THE WORD AS THE SPIRIT

There is no need to teach people how to receive the word into their mind. People do this spontaneously. However, not many Christians know how to receive the word as the Spirit. The only way to receive the word as the Spirit is by prayer. Regardless of how deeply we have received the word, it will not be life to us until we have adequate prayer. A person may hear the gospel and be very deeply inspired and moved by the Holy Spirit. However, if this person does not pray, he still cannot be saved. Regardless of how deeply this person is inspired, he still needs to pray; this is a principle. Many times we have been inspired by a good message, but we have neglected to pray. Therefore, after a short time the inspiration is gone. In order to keep the message that we have heard and been inspired by, we must immediately pray the message into our spirit. Then this message will be sown into our spirit and mingled with our spirit by our prayer. To pray makes a very big difference.

In our gospel preaching we have learned that regardless of how much people understand a message and are inspired by it, we still have to help them to pray. To pray is like putting a signature on a contract. Everything may be written into a contract, but if we do not sign it, it means nothing. From now on, after a message is delivered, we have to help the listeners to pray about it.

We can apply the same principle to our reading. Every time we read the Bible, we need to put what we have read and understood into prayer. If we spend ten minutes for reading, we should spend at least fifteen minutes for prayer. We need to pray more in order to receive what we read into our spirit. Many times when we read the word, we gain knowledge and understanding in the mind, but we are not nourished within. Not until we spend time to pray with what we read will we be nourished in our spirit. Then we will be not only enlightened and taught, but also nourished, refreshed, and strengthened within.

We have suffered too much simply because we have neglected this principle. In reading, listening, and fellowshipping we have come to know many things, and we have been truly inspired, but we have neglected to pray. Therefore, what we have heard and that which has inspired us quickly disappear. Gradually, however, we keep the knowledge in our mentality. As a result, we have much knowledge but not enough growth in life. The knowledge in our mind becomes the killing letter, which damages our Christian life.

PRAYING TO NOT QUENCH THE SPIRIT
AND TO NOT DESPISE THE MINISTERED WORD

The Epistles emphasize that we need to pray more than we need to read. First Thessalonians 5:16 through 20 says, "Always rejoice, unceasingly pray, in everything give thanks; for this is the will of God in Christ Jesus for you. Do not quench the Spirit; do not despise prophecies." If we read all these verses together, we can see that praying has very much to do with our thanksgiving to God. Verse 17 tells us to pray unceasingly, verse 18 tells us to give thanks in everything, and verse 19 says to not quench the Spirit. This implies that if we do not pray, we quench the Spirit. We may think that we quench the Spirit by doing something wrong. In actuality, we quench the Spirit simply by not praying. Moreover, verse 20 speaks of prophecies. Prophecies indicate the word and the ministry of the word. To not pray about what we have heard is to despise the ministry of the word. If we respect what we have heard in the ministry of the word, we will pray about it and pray with it.

RECEIVING THE WORD BY MEANS OF ALL PRAYER

Ephesians 6:17 and 18 say, "And receive the helmet of salvation and the sword of the Spirit, which Spirit is the word of God, by means of all prayer and petition, praying at every time in spirit and watching unto this in all perseverance and petition concerning all the saints." The context of this passage shows us that to pray is much more important than to read.

This does not mean that we should not read and listen to messages. We should do this. However, what we need is to pray more than to read. We need prayer to match our reading. We need to pray with and about every portion of the word that we read and every message we have heard. Otherwise, it can be only knowledge in the mind; it can never be nourishment and life supply in the spirit. We will have knowledge but not the Spirit. Eventually, we will have death instead of life. We all have to learn this principle. In order to have our meetings in a new and living way, we have to help the brothers and sisters to practice day by day to pray more than to read. We have neglected this too much.

SERVING AS PRIESTS BY BURNING THE INCENSE

God needs and desires a people to be priests. We are all saved to be priests (Rev. 1:6; 1 Pet. 2:5, 9). A priest is one who burns the incense before God (Exo. 30:7-8). To burn the incense is to pray. Only those who go to the Lord to pray and contact Him are those who fulfill God's purpose. In the four Gospels, when the Lord Jesus came to this earth among the Jews, there were not many priests. Rather, there were too many scribes. Scribes are religious scholars, theologians; they are not priests. Priests are not a people of knowledge. Priests are a people of incense. Day by day they burn the incense; that is, they pray. Zachariah, the father of John the Baptist, is a good example of a priest, going into the temple to burn the incense and to pray (Luke 1:8-9).

Throughout the whole Bible, even from the time of Adam, God's intention has been to have a priestly people. This is the unique kind of people that God needs. Abel was a priest, and Noah also was a priest. They did not have an official priest to make their offerings for them. They made their offerings by themselves. However, the work of the priests is not mainly to make offerings. It is to burn the incense.

There are two altars in the tabernacle. One is outside the tabernacle, and another one is inside the tabernacle. The offering altar on the outside is made of bronze, while the incense altar on the inside is of gold (Exo. 27:1-2; 30:1, 3). The offering altar is for the incense altar. We can prove this in two ways.

First, the fire used to burn the incense came from the altar of burnt offering. The only fire that could be used to burn the incense was the fire from the altar of burnt offering, the heavenly fire that came from God (Lev. 9:24). Any other kind of fire would have been "strange fire," like that which the two sons of Aaron offered (10:1). This signifies that in order to pray, we have to pray based on the redemption of the cross. Redemption at the offering altar is for fellowship at the incense altar. At the offering altar there is the cleansing of the blood for fellowship. First John 1:7 tells us that in order to maintain the fellowship, we need the cleansing of the blood. Without the offering altar we do not have the ground to burn the incense, that is, to fellowship with God. Redemption is for fellowship; it brings us back into the fellowship with God. Second, the blood shed upon the offering altar is brought into the Holy Place to be sprinkled upon the four corners of the incense altar (Lev. 4:7a). This again proves that the altar outside the tabernacle is for the one inside the Holy Place.

The priests are not those who only offer the offerings. The priests are a people that burn the incense, and to burn the incense is to pray. Ephesians 6:5 through 7 tells us that even to serve a human master as a slave is a kind of service to God. However, that is not a service like the priests had in the Holy Place when they burned the incense. Many Levites labored around the altar in the outer court, without coming into the Holy Place. They only carried the cows and sheep, slew them, skinned them, and did many other duties. That was a work to serve God, but that kind of service was different from the service of those who burned the incense. We need to learn how to burn the incense in a fine way to offer a sweet odor to God. To serve God in the outer court as a Levite is one kind of service, but to serve as a priest burning incense to God directly is another thing.

To come into the Holy of Holies is even deeper. In the Holy of Holies there is not an altar but the ark with the shekinah glory of God. The service in the outer court, the service in the Holy Place, and the service in the Holy of Holies are all services to God, but what kind of service do we want to have?

To serve in the Holy Place requires that we learn to burn the incense by praying.

OUR NEED TO PRAY IN THE SPIRIT

The tabernacle and the temple signify our being which is composed of three parts—spirit, soul, and body. In order to burn the incense, we must learn how to behave, act, and serve inwardly, not just outwardly. Gradually, we must learn how to be in our spirit. According to the record of the Bible, it is hard to discern whether the incense altar is outside the veil or within the veil before the ark (Exo. 30:6; 1 Kings 6:22; Heb. 9:3-4). This is a problem for Bible students. However, this arrangement is under God's sovereignty. In typology this signifies that when we begin to pray, we are mostly in the soul and only a little in the spirit. It is hard to tell whether we are praying in the Holy Place or in the Holy of Holies. After a few minutes, however, we enter more deeply into the spirit. At this point we are praying in the spirit.

Aaron took a censer of incense to burn before Jehovah within the veil of the tabernacle (Lev. 16:12-13). This censer is different from the incense altar. According to the proper spiritual interpretation, the incense altar is for general prayer, but the censer is for special prayers. Special prayers are something deeper, in the Holy of Holies. All our special prayers must be in the spirit. Therefore, we must learn to behave, act, live, and walk in an inward way.

OUR NEED TO CONTACT THE LORD
INWARDLY BY PRAYING

We all must seek to live in an inward way to contact the Lord. What God needs is a people to contact Him by praying. In today's Christianity there is much outward activity, but there is not much inward contact with the Lord to burn the incense. A priest is a person who burns the incense inwardly, not in the outer court but in the Holy Place, and even in the Holy of Holies, to contact the Lord. Hebrews 10:19 through 22 exhorts us to enter into the Holy of Holies, and 4:16 encourages us to touch the throne of grace. One who enters the Holy of Holies and touches the throne of grace is a priest. In

Colossians 4:16 Paul exhorted the Colossians to read his epistle to the Laodiceans, but for the most part, the writers of the Epistles encourage us not to read more but to be praying persons, persons who constantly go into the Holy of Holies to touch the throne of grace.

The kind of person who can contact God is not a working person but a praying person. What we need in the Lord's recovery today is for more people to pray. We look to the Lord for changing the way we have our meetings, but if we are not a praying people, we can have only formal meetings. We can have living meetings only when we become a praying people. We may compare the formality in Christian meetings to grave cloths. In John 11:44 the Lord told the people to remove the resurrected Lazarus's grave cloths. However, if Lazarus had not resurrected, taking off his grave cloths would only have uncovered his stench. If we change the way we meet, but our meetings are not living, they will be meetings full of stench, like a cemetery full of death. Therefore, we must encourage the brothers to learn how to pray.

PRAYING ABOUT AND WITH WHAT WE READ
TO CONTACT THE LORD

To be a praying people, every day we have to read the Word, but we have to pray more than read. If we spend ten minutes for reading, we should spend another twenty minutes for praying. This kind of prayer is not to pray for affairs, business, husbands and wives, school, jobs, or even for help. This is simply to pray about what we read and to pray with what we read in order to contact the Lord. It is not a business-doing prayer but a God-contacting prayer. We must learn to pray to feed on Christ and drink of Christ. We should forget about our business and forget about our needs. We have Matthew 6:33 as a promise: If we seek first His kingdom and His righteousness, He will add to us whatever we need. We must learn simply to seek Him by praying about what we read and with what we read.

Very few Christians have a proper prayer life, and even fewer pray with what they read. We need to pray with what we read and pray about what we read. Then the word which we receive will become the Spirit in our spirit, and when the word becomes the Spirit, it is life to us. "The words which I have spoken to you are spirit and are life" (John 6:63). How can the word become Spirit to us? There is no way other than by our prayer. May we pray about this word. May the Lord grant us a real change and a real revelation in spirit that we may serve Him, not merely in the outer court but in the Holy Place, even in the Holy of Holies. We all must learn not to be scribes or teachers but priests, paying more attention to prayer than to reading.

CHAPTER THREE

DEALING WITH CHRIST
AS THE WORD AND THE SPIRIT

Scripture Reading: John 6:57, 63; 2 Cor. 3:6b

God's intention is to mingle Himself with us and work Himself into us. The first picture in the Bible after the creation of man is that of God presenting Himself to man as the tree of life in the form of food for man to take and eat (Gen. 2:8-9). To eat is to enjoy, and whatever we enjoy by eating becomes mingled with us. God intends to offer Himself to us that we may enjoy Him all the time. In this way He can be life and everything to us and even become the very constituent of our being.

God as enjoyment to us is in Christ. Christ is the very embodiment of God; all the fullness of the Godhead dwells in Christ bodily (Col. 2:9); that is, all that God is, is embodied in Christ. Christ comes as the embodiment of God for us to take, eat, drink, and enjoy. Christ Himself told us that He came as the heavenly bread of life for us to eat and the living water for us to drink (John 6:51; 7:37-38). To eat and drink of Christ is to take Him as our enjoyment. Christ is the very embodiment of God that we may partake of and enjoy Him.

GOD EMBODIED IN CHRIST AS THE WORD
FOR OUR KNOWLEDGE OF HIM

Christ came as the embodiment of God to be enjoyed by us firstly as the Word and eventually as the Spirit. We can see this clearly in the Gospel of John. In the beginning there was Christ as the Word (1:1). The Word is the expression, definition, and revelation of God. In the Gospel of John, God is expressed and revealed through the life and walk of the Lord Jesus while He was on this earth. It is through Him that we know the fullness of God, what kind of God He is, and how He is our enjoyment. While Christ was with His disciples, the disciples heard Him, beheld Him, and handled Him (1 John 1:1). Every day they "read" the living Word. If someone were to remain with us morning to evening, day and night, we eventually would "read" him in a thorough way. For three and a half years Peter and the other disciples constantly read something of Christ, not in black and white letters but as a living Person. By the disciples' reading of Christ for three and a half years they came to know who He was.

CHRIST TRANSFIGURED INTO THE SPIRIT
FOR OUR ENJOYMENT OF HIM

However, Christ was able only to be among them. At that time He was not in them. Therefore, they were able only to know Him, not to fully enjoy Him. In order to eat something, it must be slain, cut into pieces, and cooked. Then the thing we previously only beheld will become a delicious meal to take, taste, and enjoy. This is what the Lord Jesus told the disciples after He had stayed with them for three and a half years. He told them that He would be crucified. To be crucified is to be slain, to be "put on the fire and cooked." To be cooked is to be transformed, to change into another form that can be eaten. By His crucifixion and resurrection Christ was transfigured from the flesh into the Spirit. After the four Gospels, this Word became the life-giving Spirit (1 Cor. 15:45b; 2 Cor. 3:17).

In the Epistles we do not see Christ mainly as the Word. Only 1 John 1:1 mentions Him as the Word. However, the Acts and the Epistles tell us a number of times that Christ is the Spirit. In the four Gospels Christ is the Word as the expression and revelation of God, but in the Acts and the Epistles Christ is the Spirit as our enjoyment. It is when Christ became the Spirit that He could be our enjoyment. As the Word, Christ was the revelation, but as the Spirit, He is our enjoyment, realization, and experience. When Christ was with the early disciples in the four Gospels for those three and a half years, He was a revelation to them, but He was not a realization to them since they could not experience Him. After the day of resurrection and the day of Pentecost, however, Christ was no longer only a revelation. Christ became experience to the disciples because He had become the life-giving Spirit dwelling in their spirit (Rom. 8:16; 2 Tim. 4:22), not merely for them to understand, see, and know but for them to enjoy, partake of, and experience. In order to know Christ, we have to know Him as the Word, and in order to experience Christ, we have to experience Him as the life-giving Spirit. Christ being the Word is for our knowing Him; Christ being the Spirit is for our enjoying and experiencing Him.

THREE KINDS OF SEEKERS OF CHRIST

The Fundamentalists, Seeking Christ by Studying with Their Mind

Although we may have been Christians for many years, we have mostly known Christ only as the Word. We have not enjoyed Him sufficiently as the life-giving Spirit. One kind of seeking believer studies to know Christ as the Word, making notes in his Bible, highlighting his Bible with different colors, and exercising his mind in concordances, lexicons, dictionaries, and expositions. Many times in dealing with Christ, we have exercised only our mind to study in this way.

The Pentecostals, Seeking Christ by Exercising the Gifts

Another kind of Christian says that this is too dead. This second kind of Christian seeks the Pentecostal experiences, possibly even manufacturing something in a man-made way. All of a sudden something seems to come upon him from the heavens, and he jumps, laughs, rolls, and changes his voice to speak in tongues.

Those Who Enjoy the Indwelling Christ by Exercising Their Spirit

However, not many Christians know the way of the inner life. Christ first was the Word, but after His crucifixion and resurrection, He became and still is the life-giving Spirit who is dwelling in our spirit. Now we have to exercise our human spirit as the organ with which to contact Him, experience Him, and enjoy Him in a living and inward way. The New Testament does not correspond to the way of the fundamentalists, those who only study the Word, nor to the Pentecostals, those who only seek the Pentecostal experiences. Rather, the New Testament corresponds to those who realize and enjoy that Christ today is the life-giving Spirit indwelling our spirit. We must know Him in the way revealed by 2 Timothy 4:22: "The Lord be with your spirit." We must know how to exercise our spirit to realize, enjoy, and experience Him. I do not say that we do not need the fundamental knowledge or the proper gifts. We need these. However, the fundamental knowledge and the proper gifts are for Christians to know Christ as the life-giving Spirit and experience Him by exercising their spirit to contact Him.

KNOWING HOW TO DEAL WITH CHRIST AS THE WORD AND THE SPIRIT

In the four Gospels, Christ was the Word to reveal God to us, and in the Acts and the Epistles, Christ is the life-giving Spirit for us to enjoy, contact, and experience. Therefore, we all have to know how to deal with the Word and with the Spirit. Some may know how to deal with the Word, but not in an adequate way. However, I am more concerned that many do not know how to deal with the Spirit.

We have the Bible as the Word of God, and we also have the Holy Spirit within us. These two items are the wealth, the property, that we inherit from God. If you ask me, "Brother Lee, what do you have?", I would say that I have only these two items—the Bible in my hand and the Holy Spirit in my spirit. A good Christian is one who knows how to deal with the Word and with the Spirit. In these days we have realized that we need a proper way to meet. In order to have a proper meeting, however, we need to have a proper Christian life. A proper meeting is the corporate expression and testimony of our Christian life. Moreover, in order to have a proper Christian life, we need to know how to deal with Christ as the Word and as the life-giving Spirit day by day. Until we know how to deal with Christ as the Word and the living, indwelling Spirit in an adequate way, we are not able to have a proper Christian life and a proper meeting life.

EXERCISING OUR SPIRIT
TO PRAY WITH THE WORD THAT WE READ

John 6:63 says, "The words which I have spoken to you are spirit and are life." The word has to be spirit in order to be life to us. Therefore, we must know how to transfer the word we have understood into the Spirit. If we come to the Bible only by exercising our eyes and mind to understand it, the word is still only the word. The way to transfer the word into the Spirit is by exercising our spirit to pray.

A believer may read Matthew 1:1, which says, "The book of the generation of Jesus Christ, the son of David, the son of Abraham." If he reads this verse only to try to understand it, he will receive the word only in an outward way. However, the word merely as letters brings death (2 Cor. 3:6b). Most Christians take the word only as knowledge to store in their mentality. The more we do this, though, the more death we have. This death in the mentality causes us to criticize others, and when we criticize others, we have the stench of death. However, if we transfer Matthew 1:1 into the Spirit, it becomes life. Then instead of the stench of death, this word will bear a fragrance, an incense offered to God.

When a new believer prays with Matthew 1:1, he may not know who David and Abraham are. He may simply pray, "O Lord Jesus, I do not know who David is or who Abraham is. But I do know that You, Lord, are the Son of God who became the Son of David. O Lord, You are the Son of God, but You became the Son of Man. Lord, I praise You, I adore You, and I worship You. You are God, but You became a man." If this believer reads the word in this way, he will receive not knowledge but the living Christ Himself. The more he prays in this way, the more the living Christ will be prayed into him. After reading and praying in this way for several minutes, he will be filled, satisfied, and refreshed.

There are two ways to deal with the word. One way is to ask, "Who is David? He is the father of Solomon, but who is Solomon?" This is the wrong way. This way will bring us into the forest. It may cause us to study for two weeks. Then we will be proud, knowing who David is and knowing all the things about David. We will come to the meeting to listen to the ministry of the word, carefully watching for what the speaker says about David. We may think his speaking is not accurate, so we will begin to criticize him. We may say, "This speaker has never used a good concordance. He does not have adequate knowledge. How can he come here to teach us?" This is exactly what has happened to us. Once a person who listened to me said, "This poor Brother Lee probably has never read *The Normal Christian Life*." In actuality, I heard the messages in *The Normal Christian Life* before that person was born. This illustrates how taking the word merely as letters creates knowledge, knowledge brings death, and death has its stench. May the Lord save us and deliver us from this wrong way.

The right way to receive the word is to take it as the breath of life from God (2 Tim. 3:16). This is the life food by which man lives, not by bread alone but by every word that proceeds out from the mouth of God (Matt. 4:4). This is food for the spirit, so we have to exercise our spirit to take it. To receive food for our physical body, we have to exercise our mouth, but to receive spiritual food for our spirit, we have to exercise our spirit. Whenever we come to the word, we need to realize that it is spiritual food. We must exercise our spirit to eat it, not merely to know it. We should forget about knowing and simply eat Christ. This word is the written word of the living Word. It is the expression, the revelation, of the living Word, who is Christ. He is our food, our bread of life, so whenever we come to the Bible, we come to food, not for the body but for the spirit, so we must use our spirit to take it. This is clear to us, but we have to practice to receive the word in this way, not merely to read the Bible for knowledge but to read it for feeding on it.

Genesis 1:1 says, "In the beginning God created the heavens and the earth." Most people who read this verse are tempted to know who was there in the beginning and whether the beginning was thousands, millions, or billions of years ago. This is the way to read the Bible to seek knowledge, to know by exercising the mentality. This is the wrong way. The right way to read the Bible is to exercise our spirit. If we do this, right away we will pray, "O Lord, You are the One who created all things. Everything was created by You, so everything has been initiated by You. Lord, I want You to come into my life to initiate everything." To take the word in this way is not mere knowledge. Rather, it is nourishment.

Matthew 8:1 to 3 says, "And when He came down from the mountain, great crowds followed Him. And behold, a leper, coming near, worshipped Him, saying, Lord, if You are willing, You can cleanse me. And stretching out His hand, He touched him, saying, I am willing; be cleansed! And immediately his leprosy was cleansed." Someone may take this word as knowledge and even criticize, saying that this does not sound like a proper teaching in the Bible. Rather, we should take this word by praising and praying: "Lord, come down again today to the place where I am. I am in the place of failure, in the place of leprosy, and I cannot deliver myself. Lord, if You come to the place where I am, I will be delivered. O Lord, I have been cleansed by You, but I still need You more and more. Come down, Lord, to the place where I am."

THE WORD BECOMING THE SPIRIT TO US
THROUGH OUR PRAYER

If we read the word in the morning in this way, these few verses will be a very adequate and rich breakfast. They will even be good enough for the whole week. Every day that week we can pray, "O Lord, You have come down from the mountain to the very place where I am. I have been cleansed by You. Lord, I believe, even today, that You are still coming to me. Meet me here." While we are at work, we can pray, "Lord, there is leprosy here. Come down to the place where I am." Throughout the entire day we will receive not the word only but the Lord Himself. The word will be transferred into the Spirit by our prayer. The word is black and white outside of us, but after we have prayed, it becomes the living Spirit within us, nourishing, refreshing, strengthening, and delivering us all the day.

We may further illustrate the way of life to read the word

with 1 Timothy 1:1. This verse says, "Paul, an apostle of Christ Jesus according to the command of God our Savior and of Christ Jesus our hope." A brother may read this verse, praying with praises to the Lord for being our Savior and our hope. Later in the day something disappointing may happen to him, but the more he prays, "Lord, You are my hope," the more the Spirit within him will strengthen him. In this way the word *hope* becomes the Spirit to him.

In order to pray to transfer the word into the Spirit, we must learn how to exercise, release, and uplift our spirit. Our prayer over the word also should have some understanding or inspiration in it. If we do not receive something when we start to read, then we should read further. We do not need to force ourselves to get something from every portion we read. The Bible is very rich. It is like a feast on the table. When we come to a feast, we need not force ourselves to enjoy a piece of bone that has no meat. If we were poor, we would have to break the bone to get to the marrow. However, we are not poor; the Bible is very rich. At first we may not get something from what we read, but later when we return to that same passage, we will receive something from it.

We all need to practice this way to receive the word, because we are accustomed to receiving something of knowledge. After a certain period of practice, however, we will be more accustomed to receiving something of life. Even if it is easy to get something merely of knowledge from a certain portion of the word, we would not do it. If we understand something from a portion of the word, we should not pay attention to the mere knowledge. Instead, we should receive something of life. Again I say, we need not force ourselves to get something from every portion we read. If we come to a "bone," we can forget about it for now and go on to a tender, meaty portion to get something of life. To come to the word to feast on the Lord is like coming to the dining table. We must learn to find something that we can eat.

It is too easy to get something of knowledge, but it is not as easy to get something of life. We are familiar with the bones, but we do not know the meat as well. We all must learn this proper way to read the word. This will help us to enjoy the Lord, to experience Him, and to live by Him. The Lord Jesus told us, "He who eats Me, he also shall live because of Me" (John 6:57). The proper reading of the word helps us to realize the Lord, enjoy Him, experience Him, and live by Him, and it also helps us to exercise our spirit, because in this way we pray much. Then our spirit is strengthened, uplifted, exercised, and made alive. When we come to the meetings, it will be easy to pray, because our spirit has been exercised, strengthened, and uplifted. In addition, we will have some content to pray. We will have something stored within our spirit, and our spirit will be living, because day by day we have been feeding on Christ. This is the proper, normal way for us to enjoy the Lord.

CHAPTER FOUR

FURTHER ILLUSTRATIONS OF
READING THE WORD WITH PRAYER

Prayer: Lord, under Your precious blood we come again to You. We look to You for Your help. Lord, You know that in the proper practices we need the help in the spirit. May we have the liberty and the encouragement to speak and to practice in the way of life. Do help us to this effect. We ask this in Your precious name.

NOT MAKING A FORMAL PRAYER
BUT SPEAKING TO THE LORD SPONTANEOUSLY

The more we practice to exercise our spirit to pray with the word we read, the more we will be adjusted and learn how to do it. This kind of reading will become spontaneous to us. There is no need to understand what we read and then make a formal prayer. We simply need to read something and speak to the Lord. At first, some may need to close their eyes when they pray, but after a certain amount of practice, they will become more inward and able to pray in any way.

At a certain point we will be able to read and pray with John 15:10, for example. This verse says, "If you keep My commandments, you will abide in My love; even as I have kept My Father's commandments and abide in His love." We may speak to the Lord in a spontaneous way, "Lord, not only are You Yourself life, but even Your commandment is eternal life. I do not take Your commandment merely like the Ten Commandments. I take Your commandment as life, because Your commandment is You Yourself. Lord, You told us clearly that without You we can do nothing. I take simply Your commandment as Yourself. You are joy, and You are love." There is no need to make a formal prayer. We may simply speak with the Lord in this way.

When we talk to the Lord in this way, we should not exercise our mind too much. Rather, we need to learn to exercise our spirit to open deeply from within and speak something to the Lord. We need more practice. When we start to practice to read and pray in this way, we will need to set aside some definite time each day. After we are more accustomed to this, however, we can do it throughout the entire day. The word will be familiar to us, and we will be able to turn any verse into prayer. Then each verse will become the Spirit to us. We need more practice to become accustomed to this.

TURNING EVERY PASSAGE INTO PRAYER
BY EXERCISING OUR SPIRIT

We need to read the Bible without exercising our choice. We should begin from Matthew 1:1 and simply continue to read in order. One day we can read the first eight verses, and the next day we can continue from verse 9 and read another five or ten verses. One morning we may come to Mark 4:3 to 6, which says, "Listen! Behold, the sower went out to sow. And as he sowed, some seed fell beside the way, and the birds came and devoured it. And other seed fell on the rocky place, where it did not have much earth, and immediately it sprang up because it had no depth of earth. And when the sun rose, it was scorched; and because it had no root, it withered." We can pray something simple without much doctrine and without "ministering a message" in our prayer. Spontaneously we may say, "Lord, I praise You that You are the sower and You are the seed. O Lord, You have sown Yourself into me. Oh, the seed! You are the seed." Sometimes we may repeat several times, "O Lord, You are the wonderful seed." Then we may come to our spouse and say, "Dear wife, the Lord is the seed!" We can also turn to the enemy and say, "Satan, do you not know that the Lord is the seed within me?"

This is a simple and living way to pray without many words. Sometimes our prayers are too wordy. Many words are piled together, but there is nothing of substance. Our prayer over Mark 4 can simply be: "Lord, You are the living seed, the seed of life that has been sown into me. I praise You that by Your mercy I am not by the wayside. I am afraid, though, that I may have some stones. My heart may be the stony earth. Lord, show me the stones and take them away. Grant that You may grow deeply within me." Such a prayer is living; it is not in the exercise of the mind. We have to exercise our spirit to say something to the Lord in a living way from deep within. This requires our practice.

BY OUR TRANSFERRING THE WORD INTO THE SPIRIT, THE BIBLE BECOMING A "DIFFERENT" BOOK TO US

We need to change our way of reading the word. We must take the word as truth, not merely as knowledge, and realize that the word must be transferred into the Spirit. This is the right principle. In order for the word to apply to us, we have to know the way to transfer the word into the Spirit. Many people read the Bible but receive no supply. They increase in knowledge but have no growth in life. In order to have the growth in life, we must realize the proper way to transfer the word into the Spirit. Eventually the Bible will truly be open to us in the way of life. It will become a different book to us. Brother Watchman Nee once said that different people have different Bibles. It is not that the Bible changes; the Bible is the same. Yours has sixty-six books, and so does mine. Yours begins with Genesis and ends with Revelation, and mine does too. However, our experience of the Bible is different. The kind of Bible we have depends on what kind of person we are and how we read it.

I heard Brother Nee speak this word a long time ago, but gradually in my experience I have come to realize that it is true. Once a brother came to me and said, "The Bible is truly good." I asked him, "What do you mean?" He said, "In the whole world there is not another book like this which teaches that wives have to submit to their husband." I found out that this brother had a problem with his wife. He always expected his wife to be submissive to him, and he became a Christian for this purpose. He told us that we should send some sisters to his home to help his wife with this teaching. This illustrates that if we are a certain kind of person, the Bible will be a certain kind of book to us. What kind of Bible we have depends on what kind of person we are. The same Bible may have been a certain book to us five years ago and be another kind of book today. If we practice the proper way to pray with what we read, the Bible will "change" after only six months. It will be another book. We need this practice in order to receive the word in the way of life.

TAKING THE LORD'S PROMISES BY PRAYING

Certain parts of the word are a promise. Isaiah 54:1 and 2 are a promise to the barren. They say, "Give a ringing shout, O barren one, you who have not borne; / Break forth into joyful shouting and cry out, you who have not been in labor; / For more numerous are the children of the desolate one / Than the children of the married woman, says Jehovah. / Enlarge your tent site, / Let them stretch out the curtains of your habitations; / Spare not; / Lengthen your cords, / And strengthen your pegs." When we read this, we may pray in a brief way with a strong spirit to take the Lord's promise: "Lord, I take Your word as a promise to me. I myself cannot break forth into singing, but You can do it. My tent site is my spirit. Lord, enlarge it. Enlarge it and stretch out the curtains of my habitations." Keep this word as the promise of the Lord and spend some time to pray over it. If we deal with the Lord in this way, the Holy Spirit will give us living utterances. Then the more we speak them, the more we will taste, enjoy, and absorb not mere knowledge but the Lord Himself as life and nourishment.

READING THE WORD IN A NEW WAY, THE WAY OF LIFE

This is the right way to read the word. It is absolutely something different from the old way. The old way to read is the natural way, the way in which people read any common, published material. The way that the children of God read the living word must be different. It must not be natural and religious but spiritual and living.

We may further illustrate reading the word by praying with Isaiah 15:1. This verse begins, "The burden concerning Moab: Indeed in a night it is devastated." When we read this, again we may pray, "Lord, I do not know what Moab is, but I know that the city in which I presently live can be like Moab. Lord, grant me a burden for this city." We can simply pray to the extent of our spiritual understanding. Then the Scripture will be not just a word or some knowledge but something living. Many times through this kind of prayer the Lord will do something. The Lord will hear and answer our prayer and grant us to be burdened for the city in which we live. From that time on we will have a real burden day by day. Even while we are working or driving, we will pray with tears for our city.

There is a great difference between the way of knowledge and the way of life to realize the word, to make the word living in the spirit. What we have is the living word of God. To come to the word properly always paves the way for the Holy Spirit to come in. If we practice to come to the word properly, the Holy Spirit will come in, and many things will result in a living way. Let us open the way for the Holy Spirit to do many wonderful things. What we are reading is not the word in dead letters; it is something living.

First Timothy 6:1 says, "As many as are slaves under the yoke should regard their own masters as worthy of all honor, lest the name of God and our teaching be blasphemed." Since we are not this kind of slave, we may have no inspiration to pray with this verse. We should not force ourselves to get something from it. Rather, we may leave this verse for now and continue to read. However, sometimes we may be inspired by this kind of passage. We may have the realization that the Lord is the Master; we have to serve Him honestly and faithfully. If we have this kind of sense, we should turn it into prayer. Again I say, do not formulate a prayer. Instead, simply have a spontaneous talk with the Lord. If we compose a prayer, we will drift into the mind. We must always avoid exercising our mind in this way. We should be simple to speak from the depths of our being, to say something from the spirit. We may say, "O Lord, although I am not this kind of slave, I am Your slave, and You are my Master. I want to serve You honestly."

TAKING THE WORD BY PRAYER
REQUIRING OUR PRACTICE

Someone may ask, "If I do not compose a prayer, how can I pray?" This requires our practice. Eventually we will arrive at the point when we simply pray without composing. When we have a family talk, we do not compose anything; we simply talk. We need to practice talking to the Lord while we read His word. Without thinking, considering, or composing we simply speak from the spirit: "O Lord, I do not have an earthly master, but I do have You as my Master."

With everything there is the need of practice, and this matter is no exception. We need to practice to exercise our spirit and train our faculties to be accustomed to this kind of reading and praying. We look to the Lord. From now on we all have to learn this way to contact the word and to transfer the word into the Spirit. Then we will enjoy the Lord and always pray in the spirit. Our spirit will be strengthened, enlarged, and enlivened. Then when we come together to meet, we will have a strong, living spirit and the accumulation of divine content within us.

CHAPTER FIVE

CHRIST AS THE WORD BECOMING THE SPIRIT TO BE ENJOYED BY US

Scripture Reading: John 1:1, 14, 18; 14:16-20; Acts 9:4; Rom. 8:9-11; 1 Cor. 6:17; 15:45b; 2 Cor. 3:17; 4:7; 13:5; Gal. 1:16; 2:20; 4:19; 6:18; Eph. 3:16-17; Phil. 1:19; Col. 1:27; 3:4, 11; Rev. 2:1, 7, 8, 11; 5:6; 22:1-2

We need to have a full view of the Lord Jesus as the Word and as the Spirit. The four Gospels are a full record, picture, and revelation of the Lord Jesus as the expression of God, the Word of God for us to "read," see, and understand (John 1:1, 14, 18). In order to know who and what the Lord Jesus is, we have to spend time to study the four Gospels. In these four books the Lord Jesus is revealed to us in many aspects. In reading the four Gospels, we should pay attention not mainly to what He did, but to go further to see what He is. By His doing, His being is revealed. Mainly, we need to learn what He is and who He is.

The four Gospels—Matthew, Mark, Luke, and John—give us a full picture of this wonderful Christ as the Word, the expression and revelation of God. After the Gospels is the second part of the New Testament—the Acts and the Epistles. In this part the Lord Jesus is revealed not only as the Word but as the Spirit (1 Cor. 15:45b; 2 Cor. 3:17). As the Word, Christ is in the stage of revelation, expression, and explanation, and as the Spirit, He is in the stage of enjoyment and experience. Therefore, after we know Christ as the Word, we have to enjoy Him as the Spirit.

We need to be able to show people how Christ is revealed in the Gospels as the Word, not the Spirit, and how He is revealed in the Epistles not mainly as the Word but as the

Spirit. To adequately study the New Testament with this in view may require one or two years. Too many Christians today have a weak point in that they know spiritual things only in a superficial way, merely repeating what others say but not knowing how to demonstrate what they say from the Scriptures. This is not right. Scientists today study things from their fundamentals. They become experts and can answer questions in detail. In the same way, and especially since we are taking the way of the Lord's recovery, we cannot simply repeat what others say. We have to thoroughly know the truth concerning Christ as the Word and the Spirit and be able to give adequate answers concerning it. The light, confirmation, and adequate, proper, and strong proofs of this truth should flow out of us like a waterfall.

In the Epistles no one asks who the Lord is. In the four Gospels, however, the Lord asked the disciples, "Who do men say that the Son of Man is?" (Matt. 16:13). The disciples answered, "Some, John the Baptist; and others, Elijah; and still others, Jeremiah or one of the prophets," to which the Lord asked, "But you, who do you say that I am?" (vv. 14-15). This passage is a strong proof that in the four Gospels the Lord is the Word, the revelation of God, for people to know Him. At other times in the Gospels the disciples would ask, "What kind of man is this?" (8:27). In the Epistles, however, we cannot find this kind of question. Rather, there is another category of expressions concerning Christ, because in the Epistles Christ is revealed as the Spirit.

Today most Christians are in the stage of the four Gospels. Many know Christ as the Word in the four Gospels, but they do not know Christ in the stage of the Epistles. Because of this, many hold only the doctrine and teaching concerning the Lord Jesus. They can say, "Christ is God, and He is man" merely with their knowledge, but they have few experiences of Christ. On the other hand, some who have a certain experience of Christ do not have an adequate understanding. They claim that they have the experience of Christ by the "help of the Holy Spirit." It is as if they are saying, "I am here on this earth, and Christ is there in the heavens. We are too far apart. It is the Holy Spirit that helps me to contact Christ." In their understanding, Christ and the Holy Spirit are separate, the Holy Spirit being only a help and means. This is a wrong concept and understanding. Most Christians today do not see that Christ is the Spirit (2 Cor. 3:17; cf. 4:5). In order to experience Christ, we have to experience the Spirit, because Christ is the Spirit.

THE GOSPELS BEING AN EXPLANATION AND REVELATION OF CHRIST

The Gospel of Matthew begins with the genealogy of Christ. A genealogy is an explanation of a person, telling us who he is. Therefore, on the first page of the New Testament is an explanation, a revelation, of the person of Christ, telling us who He is. According to the principle of first mention, this establishes that the subject of the Gospels is the person of Christ. Immediately after this is the record of the birth of this person. The first two things we need to know about a person are his genealogy and birth. When we fill out papers about our status, we have to tell people about our parents, nationality, and date and place of birth. This shows us again that the Gospels tell us who Christ is and what kind of person He is.

After His genealogy and birth, the Gospels present the recommendation of Christ by His forerunner, John the Baptist. A recommendation is a revelation, a certain kind of explanation telling us who a person is. In today's business and society we always need a reference. The Gospels give us a reference to prove and to recommend who Christ is. Following this is a test, a temptation, to prove what kind of person Christ is. In this way each page of the Gospels proves one thing: what kind of person this One is.

Although His testing proved who Christ is, we still need some practical illustrations and explanations, such as the accounts in Matthew 8, 15, and eventually 17, where Christ was suddenly transfigured on the mountain. We do not have this kind of record in the Epistles. When we come to the Epistles, the picture changes. The Gospels and the Epistles present two different kinds of pictures of Christ.

Matthew, Mark, and Luke are all of one category. In these three Gospels, Christ is revealed as a man. In the first

Gospel, He as a man is the King committed with all authority. In the second book, as a man He is a slave serving not only God but also us, with power, love, and even His own life. In the third book, as a perfect man He is the Savior, who went into death to redeem us. The last book of the Gospels is in another category. The Gospel of John tells us, "In the beginning was the Word" (1:1). This Gospel tells us that Christ was the Word, and the Word was God. Here Christ is revealed as God incarnate who came to impart life to us. In this way, the four Gospels present a picture and a record of all the aspects of Christ as the Word, showing us who this person is and what kind of person He is. All the records in chapter after chapter have only this one purpose. To read these four Gospels is simply to read an explanation and a definition of a person.

However, in the Gospels Christ is not yet the Spirit. He was among people to be seen, understood, and apprehended, but He could not come into people for them to enjoy. People could appreciate Him, admire Him, and praise Him, but they could not share of Him and partake of Him. People could understand Him as the Word, but until the Word became the Spirit He could not come into them.

JOHN 14 BEING THE TURNING POINT IN THE STAGES OF CHRIST

For this reason, we cannot find a verse or passage in the four Gospels that tells us that Christ is the Spirit or that Christ is in the disciples, until we come to John 14 and 15. However, John 14 and 15 speak of Christ related not merely to the stage of the four Gospels. What these chapters refer to does not happen in the Gospels. They predict something about Christ in the stage of the Epistles. Similarly, John 20 takes place in the Gospels, but this chapter may be considered as the end of the stage of the Gospels and the beginning of the stage of the Epistles.

It was through His death and resurrection that Christ as the Word became the Spirit. That is why John 14 tells us that He had to go through death and be resurrected. It is from this chapter that the Spirit is first mentioned so clearly. Verses 16 and 17 say, "And I will ask the Father, and He will give you another Comforter, that He may be with you forever, even the Spirit of reality, whom the world cannot receive, because it does not behold Him or know Him; but you know Him, because He abides with you and shall be in you." Christ was the first Comforter, but He would send another Comforter, the Paraclete, the Spirit of reality.

Verse 17 says that this Spirit was abiding with the disciples and would be in them. To be in them indicated a further step. The Word was among them already, because the Word became flesh and tabernacled among them (1:14). However, the disciples needed the Lord's second step so that He could become the Spirit to be not only among them but in them. Verse 17 of chapter fourteen says concerning the Spirit, "He abides with you and shall be in you," but right away verse 18 says "I will not leave you as orphans; I am coming to you." *He* in verse 17 changes into *I* in verse 18. Christ's going in death and resurrection was His coming as the Spirit to be in the disciples.

Verses 19 and 20 continue, "Yet a little while and the world beholds Me no longer, but you behold Me; because I live, you also shall live. In that day you will know that I am in My Father, and you in Me, and I in you." At that time He could only be among the disciples; He could not be in them. In "that day," however, He would be in them. These are the two steps of Christ—to be incarnated in the flesh to be among the disciples and to be transfigured into the Spirit to be in the disciples.

As the turning point in these two steps, John 14 is the most significant chapter in the entire Bible. It is in this portion of the Word that we have the Spirit of reality, the Spirit as the reality of Christ, and it is in this portion of the Word that we have the phrase *in you*. In the entire Bible before this chapter the phrase *in you* was never used in this way. Then in the following chapter the Lord says, "Abide in me and I in you" (15:4). If Christ were only the Word, how could He abide in us? To abide in us He must be the Spirit. It is at this turning point that the Word became the Spirit through crucifixion and resurrection. Therefore, after His resurrection He is no longer only the Word; rather, He is mainly the Spirit. As the Spirit He can be in us, and He truly is in us.

THE ACTS SHOWING US THE FACT OF CHRIST
BEING IN THE DISCIPLES

Apparently there is no verse in the Acts that tells us that Christ was in Peter, John, James, or Stephen. However, in Acts there is the fact to prove that Christ was not only in the disciples but even one with them. When Christ revealed Himself to Saul of Tarsus, He said, "Saul, Saul, why are you persecuting Me?" (9:4). It is as if the Lord was saying, "When you persecute Stephen and My other disciples, you persecute Me, because I am one with them. I suffer your persecution within them." Here is the fact that Christ was one with all His disciples, because Christ as the living Spirit was in all His disciples.

THE EPISTLES TELLING US
THAT CHRIST AS THE SPIRIT IS IN US

In the Epistles, Romans 8:9 to 11 tells us that Christ is in us. This passage speaks of the Spirit of God, the Spirit of Christ, and Christ Himself interchangeably. The Spirit of God is the Spirit of Christ, and the Spirit of Christ is Christ Himself. This passage makes it very clear that Christ now is the Spirit. Therefore, whatever Romans 8 says about the Spirit, it is speaking about Christ as the Spirit. The Spirit mentioned in Romans 8 is nothing less or different than Christ Himself. Christ as the Spirit is living in every saved person.

Following this, 1 Corinthians 6:17 says, "He who is joined to the Lord is one spirit." This is a strong proof that the Lord is the Spirit. If He were not the Spirit, how could we be one spirit with Him? This is also a strong proof that we have a human spirit and that Christ as the Spirit is in our spirit, so that we can be one spirit with Him. First Corinthians also uses the phrase *in Christ* a number of times (1:2, 4, 30; 4:15, 17; 15:22; 16:24). Finally, 15:45b says, "The last Adam became a life-giving Spirit."

Several passages in 2 Corinthians show us that Christ is in us. Verse 17 of chapter three says, "The Lord is the Spirit," and 4:7 says that Christ is the treasure in us, the earthen vessels. At the end of the book, 13:5 says, "Test yourselves whether you are in the faith; prove yourselves. Or do you not realize about yourselves that Jesus Christ is in you, unless you are disapproved?"

Galatians 1:16, 2:20, and 4:19 tell us that Christ is in us, and the last verse, 6:18, says, "The grace of our Lord Jesus Christ be with your spirit, brothers." Next, Ephesians 3:16 and 17 is a prayer that our inner man be strengthened and that Christ would make His home in our heart. Philippians 1:19 speaks of the bountiful supply of the Spirit of Jesus Christ, who was in the apostle Paul. Colossians 1:27 says, "Christ in you, the hope of glory," 3:4 speaks of "Christ our life," and verse 11 says, "Christ is all and in all." In the same way, we can also find verses like these throughout the remainder of the Epistles. These are just a few of the verses that show us that Christ as the Spirit lives in us. There is no need to glean this kind of passage; there is a full harvest of these passages in the New Testament.

REVELATION REVEALING
THE SPEAKING CHRIST AS THE SPEAKING SPIRIT
AND THE REDEEMING CHRIST AS THE FLOWING SPIRIT

Each of the seven epistles in Revelation 2 and 3 begins with, "These things says," referring to the Lord Himself in His various qualifications (2:1, 8, 12, 18; 3:1, 7, 14), but the end of every epistle says, "...hear what the Spirit says to the churches" (2:7, 11, 17, 29; 3:6, 13, 22). Revelation 2:1, for example, says, "To the messenger of the church in Ephesus write: These things says He who holds the seven stars in His right hand, He who walks in the midst of the seven golden lampstands." *Says He* means "Christ says." However, the end of the epistle says, "He who has an ear, let him hear what the Spirit says to the churches" (v. 7). By this we can see that "He" is "the Spirit," and "the Spirit" is "He."

Likewise, verse 8 says, "And to the messenger of the church in Smyrna write: These things says the First and the Last, who became dead and lived again." The one speaking here is Christ. However, verse 11 begins, "He who has an ear, let him hear what the Spirit says to the churches." The beginning of every epistle says that the Lord speaks, but the end of each epistle says that the Spirit speaks. The Spirit is the Lord, and the Lord is the Spirit.

Revelation 5:6 says, "And I saw in the midst of the throne and of the four living creatures and in the midst of the elders a Lamb standing as having just been slain, having seven horns and seven eyes, which are the seven Spirits of God sent forth into all the earth." The Lord as the Lamb has seven eyes, and the seven eyes are the seven Spirits. That indicates that Christ comes to us as the seven eyes, that is, as the Spirit, for us to experience. Moreover, the Lamb is on the throne, from the throne flows the river of water of life, and in the water of life grows the tree of life (22:1-2). This is a picture of the redeeming Christ, who has become the life-giving Spirit constantly flowing with the life supply.

By all this, we can see that Christ is no longer only the Word but the life-giving Spirit, not only for us to know and understand, but for us to enjoy, take, and experience. We cannot enjoy Christ only by knowing Him as the Word. We have to enjoy Christ by realizing Him as the Spirit. Therefore, we must not exercise only our mind to understand Him; we have to exercise our spirit to contact Him in our spirit, as revealed in the Epistles.

CHAPTER SIX

EATING THE WORD BY READING AND PRAYING

Scripture Reading: Col. 3:16; Eph. 5:18-20; Matt. 4:4; Jer. 15:16; Exo. 30:7-8

THE CHRISTIAN LIFE
BEING A LIFE OF ENJOYING CHRIST

Colossians 3:16 says, "Let the word of Christ dwell in you richly in all wisdom, teaching and admonishing one another with psalms and hymns and spiritual songs, singing with grace in your hearts to God." Psalms are the longest songs, hymns are shorter, and spiritual songs are the shortest ones, like choruses. Verse 17 continues, "And whatever you do in word or in deed, do all things in the name of the Lord Jesus, giving thanks to God the Father through Him." The issue of this is in verses 18 through 20: "Wives, be subject to your husbands, as is fitting in the Lord. Husbands, love your wives and do not be bitter against them. Children, obey your parents in all things, for this is well pleasing in the Lord." Then the subsequent verses go on to speak of fathers, slaves, and masters. This indicates that all the proper things in the Christian life—such as wives submitting to their husbands, husbands loving their wives, children being under their parents, slaves serving properly, and masters treating their slaves rightly—all come out of the enjoyment of the Lord through the word in praising and thanking.

According to the context of these verses, we first have the word as the means to convey Christ to us, and we enjoy Him to such an extent that we are filled with Him. Then praises and thanks flow out like living water. From this kind of enjoyment of the Lord, submission issues from wives, love comes out from husbands, and honor for parents comes out from the children. All these different matters in the Christian walk issue out of the enjoyment of Christ.

Ephesians 5:18 through 20 confirms this same truth. These verses say, "And do not be drunk with wine, in which is dissoluteness, but be filled in spirit, speaking to one another in psalms and hymns and spiritual songs, singing and psalming with your heart to the Lord, giving thanks at all times for all things in the name of our Lord Jesus Christ to our God and Father." Colossians 3:16 tells us to be filled with the word, while Ephesians 5 tells us to be filled in spirit. Verses 21 and 22 continue, "Being subject to one another in the fear of Christ: Wives, be subject to your own husbands as to the Lord." Following this, Ephesians 6 continues by speaking of children, fathers and mothers, and slaves and masters (vv. 1-9). This is the same as Paul's word in Colossians, again showing that all the proper matters of the Christian life come out of the infilling and enjoyment of the Lord.

Many Christians seem to cut off the portion concerning being filled in spirit and pick up only the portion that teaches the wives to submit to their own husbands, the husbands to love their wives, and the children, parents, slaves, and masters to be proper. However, all these things in the Christian walk issue from the enjoyment of Christ. When we are filled with Christ and enjoying Christ to the fullest extent, something flows out from this filling within. The submission of a wife and the love of a husband are outflows from the inner filling. The matter of foremost importance in Colossians 3 and Ephesians 5 is the enjoyment of Christ. If we are filled with Christ, all these other things come out spontaneously.

The Christian life is not a religious life or even merely a moral life. The Christian life is simply a life of enjoying Christ all the time. All the proper and necessary matters come out from and depend upon this enjoyment. Even the church life itself is a matter of the enjoyment of Christ. If we do not have the enjoyment of Christ, it is hard to have the church life. We can have a certain kind of religion or organization, but we cannot have the church life. The church life is the overflow of the enjoyment of Christ. This is proven in the last part of Ephesians 5, which speaks of the church (v. 32). When we all enjoy Christ to the fullest extent, the church life comes into being.

ENJOYING CHRIST BY TAKING THE WORD AS FOOD

God's intention is to give Himself to us as our enjoyment in Christ through the Spirit. Therefore, we have to know how to enjoy Christ. Then we will have the proper Christian life. Both the Christian life and the church life depend on one thing: the enjoyment of Christ. To enjoy God in Christ is simply to deal with two things—the word and the Spirit. We have the holy Bible in our hands, and we have the Holy Spirit in our spirit. Both the holy Bible and the Holy Spirit are the means for us to enjoy Christ. Christ is the Word, and He is the Spirit. Therefore, in order to enjoy Christ we have to deal with the word and the Spirit.

There are two different ways to read the word. One way is to read the word but not contact Christ. Too many Christians read the word without ever contacting Christ. This is the wrong way. The right way to read the word is to realize that the word is not mainly for knowledge but for food. "Man shall not live on bread alone, but on every word that proceeds out through the mouth of God" (Matt. 4:4). Jeremiah 15:16 says, "Your words were found and I ate them." We need to eat the word, because the word is food.

Physical food is for our body, so we have to eat it with our body and take it into our body. In the same principle, the word is spiritual food, food for the spirit, so we have to eat it with our spirit and take it into our spirit. We all have to learn how to take the word by our spirit and into our spirit. There is no other way to do this but by praying. We must pray over, pray about, and pray with whatever we read and understand. This is something that is very much overlooked by Christians today. Many Christians read the Bible, but not many read the Bible in this way.

We need to buy physical food, prepare it by cooking, and set aside fifteen to twenty-five minutes to eat it. We should not eat too fast. We need the adequate time to eat properly. We can rush into a supermarket to buy something hastily, and we can throw something on the stove quickly, but we cannot throw something into our stomach too quickly. We need the time to chew and eat in a fine way. In the same way, we need some time day by day to take the word finely, not by exercising our mind to understand but by exercising our innermost part, our spirit. To take the word in this way, we need to pray over what we read and understand, that is, to pray-read. We must learn to pray, not in a formal way by composing a prayer but in an informal way, just as we talk with our loved ones.

Sometimes we may need to read the Bible to gain some knowledge of the Bible. We may also need to go to the dictionary to learn the meaning of new words that we find. However, this is not the main way to deal with the word. The main thing we need is to take twenty to thirty minutes, at least once a day, although three times is better, to deal with the word not merely to know it but to eat it, digest it, and transfer it into the Spirit. Do not say that you have no time to do this. If you do not have the time to spend in the word, it is better not to spend your time on a physical meal. Rather, spend one physical meal time for a spiritual meal. Do not be afraid that you will be short of one meal. I assure you that you will be more healthy. In order to be spiritually healthy, we need to take at least one spiritual meal day by day.

We cannot expect a brother to be normal and healthy in his Christian life if he does not know how to eat the Lord by dealing with the word. Regardless of how many messages we give people and of how good those messages are, if those who hear them do not know how to eat the Lord, drink the Lord, and feast on the Lord, the messages will not work for them. We may have messages on the cross and about many other things, but we still need to feed on the Lord, drink of Him, and feast on Him. This is of the greatest importance. I hope that we all will practice this day by day, especially in the morning. We need to spend at least ten minutes with the Lord to feast on Him by eating the word.

THE PRACTICAL WAY TO EAT THE WORD

The way to eat the word is first not to read too much. Our

time in the word is not to buy something from the supermarket; it is to eat a breakfast. Therefore, we should not take too much, just an adequate portion. Second, we should not try to understand too much. At other times we may need to exercise our mind by reading, but our time for eating the word is not for exercising our mind. We should simply read and understand whatever we can understand. We need not try to understand more than that; this will frustrate us. If we read a few verses or even half of a chapter and do not understand it, we should leave it and continue to read. Perhaps in the following verses we will understand something.

Third, once we understand something, we should ponder over it a little. I do not like to use the word *meditate,* because that word has been wrongly used. Sometimes to meditate is merely to exercise the mind. In that case, it is better not to meditate. When some Christians meditate too much, they travel throughout the whole Bible, from Genesis to Revelation, back to the Psalms, and then back to Genesis. That does not help. However, when we are inspired with something from the word, we should consider it.

Then, fourth, right away we should pray over what we understand. It is by this kind of prayer that we have a fresh contact not only with the word but also with the Lord Himself through the word. Eventually, the Lord and the word, the word and the Lord, become one to us. In this way, our prayer and reading will be mingled. While we read and consider, we speak something to the Lord, and while we are speaking something to the Lord, we ponder on the word and consider what we understand. This is praying and reading, reading and praying, mingled together.

Matthew 8:1 to 4 says that the Lord Jesus "came down from the mountain" and healed a leper. When we read this portion, we may be inspired that the Lord came down from the mountain. Then we can say, "I praise You, Lord, that You have come down from the mountain. You have come down to the place where I am. O Lord, come down once again today that I may be healed. If You come, my leprosy will go away." It may not be possible to read and pray in this way for an hour, but to take twenty minutes is possible. Try to do this in the morning and again during the day. I would suggest, especially to the young ones, that you keep a small Bible in your pocket. Throughout the day or during recess or rest you can open it and read two or three verses. Then you will get something, and you can pray over it.

Some may ask, "How can I read and pray? If I read, I have to open my eyes, but if I pray, I have to close them." Forget about opening or closing your eyes. If you need to close your eyes, close them spontaneously, but if you do not need to close them, do not make that a form. Even when we close our eyes, we still can "read," because the word has already gotten into us.

It is very convenient to have the word within us. Many times people do not realize that I am reading the word, because I am not reading a Bible outwardly. However, many times I "read" inwardly. I recall Romans 8:1 and 2: "There is now then no condemnation to those who are in Christ Jesus. For the law of the Spirit of life has freed me in Christ Jesus from the law of sin and of death." Spontaneously I say to the Lord, "Praise You, I am in Christ. Hallelujah, I am not in Los Angeles; I am in Christ!" When I am bothered by something, I say, "I am not in this place. I am in Christ. Praise the Lord! Hallelujah! I am in Christ." We have to be beside ourselves in this way, to say, "Oh, praise the Lord, the Spirit of life! O Lord, You are the Spirit of life, and this life-giving Spirit is in me. With this Spirit there is the liberating law, setting me free from the law of sin and of death." We can also turn to the enemy and say, "Satan, I am not afraid of you any more. I have another One who is stronger than you. If you come to fight with me, you will be defeated." This is the living way to read the word.

READING AND PRAYING TO BE FILLED
WITH THE WORD AND WITH THE SPIRIT

Ten minutes before dinner is served, we can come to the word to read and pray. By the time dinner comes, we already will have had a good meal, eating the word and feeding on the Lord. Try this; you will see the difference in your Christian life. Your Christian life will be different from what you had in the past. You will know how to feed on the Lord and feed on the word. Eventually, you will be filled with the word and with the Spirit. It will be hard to differentiate between the word and the Spirit. In Colossians 3:16 the word of Christ fills us, but in Ephesians 5:18 we are filled in spirit. These two—the word and the Spirit—are one. When we are filled with the word, we are filled with the Spirit.

It is wrong to be filled with the word but not with the Spirit. Do not forget this formula: "The word without the Spirit is knowledge. Knowledge without life is death. When death becomes old, it has a stench." Always reading without eating, without praying, merely amasses knowledge in letters. The letter kills (2 Cor. 3:6), and death brings its stench. Therefore, we have to transfer the word into the Spirit. Whenever we have the Spirit, we have life, and when we have life, we have a sweet fragrance. The sweet odor of Christ will constantly spread within us (2 Cor. 2:15). The secret, the key, is to transfer the word to the Spirit by praying. This does not mean that we should not read and study the word to gain knowledge. We all need to do this, just as we need to go to the supermarket to buy groceries and store them up. However, that is not all. We need to eat.

We may know much about the Bible, but how much have we eaten? This is the problem among Christians. We are not accustomed to eating, so we must now learn how to do it. This is why I have a burden to stress the matter of our eating. If someone does not have the desire to eat, he is sick. Only sick people do not have an appetite. Such a one must pray that the Lord would cure him. Healthy Christians, however, must practice to eat. Even if you feel you are clear about this, you still need more practice.

NOT NEEDING TO UNDERSTAND EVERYTHING WE READ, NOT READING TOO QUICKLY, AND NOT COMPOSING FORMAL PRAYERS

Psalm 35:1 and 2 say, "Strive, O Jehovah, with those who strive with me; / Battle against those who battle against me. / Take hold of buckler and shield, / And rise up as my help." It is not very easy to apply a passage like this, except if under the Lord's sovereignty we have a case like the psalmist's. If we do not have such a case, we need not apply these two verses to ourselves. We should not try to force anything. If there is something in verses like these to digest, then we can digest it. Otherwise, we can simply go on to the following verses. There is no need to get something from every verse. The Bible is very rich; if we continue to read, we will get something eventually. It might be that on one morning we receive nothing from a particular passage, but a few months later when we have the need, the Spirit will bring it back to our understanding. At that time we can pray in a better way.

When we eat physical food, we should not swallow it too quickly. We have to chew it for a certain amount of time. In the same way, when we read and pray with the word, we should not read too quickly, and neither should we compose formal prayers. We simply should read and talk to the Lord in a spontaneous way. When I was young, I was very religious. Whenever I prayed, I felt I had to kneel down and speak properly. This was too religious and formal. Later I realized that the Lord does not honor this. Rather, He honors that we know how to contact Him and eat Him. On the one hand, we should not be light, loose, and wild, but on the other hand, we should forget about formality and religion and simply be spontaneous. Sometimes we may read the word in the garden or in the car, sometimes we may sit to read and speak to the Lord, and at other times we may have to kneel down to read and speak to the Lord. We simply should contact the Lord by talking with Him in a very spontaneous way, yet in the spirit, to absorb Him by reading and praying, that is, by talking to the Lord based on what we have read and understood.

THE WORD BECOMING THE SPIRIT
DEALING WITH ALL OUR PROBLEMS

If we try to do this, we will see the difference in our Christian life. Many problems will be solved spontaneously by this kind of eating, because we will digest many spiritual "vitamins" that deal with the problems and swallow up death. There are many problems that we cannot solve and that no one can help us to solve. Likewise, there are many questions that no one can answer for us. However, simply by feasting on the Lord in this way, the inner supply and nourishment will take care of all our problems. The nourishment will solve the problems. The vitamins will meet the need and kill the germs.

At one time I felt that I had a problem with my eyes. By the evening time it was hard for me to see or to read. When I contacted an eye specialist, he told me that I needed to eat something with vitamin A. I said to him, "There is something wrong with my seeing. Why are you talking to me about eating?" He laughed and said, "Just go buy some vitamins or cod liver oil pills and take them daily. After three days you will see the difference." I learned from that experience. The problem was not that I could not see; the problem was that I was short of vitamin A. In the same principle, many problems in our Christian life are due to one thing—we are short of Christ. I do not mean that we are short of the knowledge of Christ. We may have too much knowledge of Christ. We are short not of the "prescription" but of the "vitamin" itself. We simply need to take more Christ. Then we will be well. Do not argue with this; simply go to try it. Then you will be thankful for this word.

LIGHTING THE LAMPS AND BURNING THE INCENSE

In the type of the tabernacle, dealing with the lamps and burning the incense go together. Exodus 30:7 and 8 say, "And Aaron shall burn on it fragrant incense; every morning when he dresses the lamps he shall burn it. And when Aaron sets up the lamps at twilight, he shall burn it, a perpetual incense before Jehovah throughout your generations." In the morning the priest burned the incense when he dressed the lamps, and in the evening he burned the incense again when he set up the lamps. Moreover, the incense was not for one day, one month, one year, or one generation only; it was a constant, continual, perpetual incense before Jehovah throughout all generations. This means that all day as we deal with the lamps, we need to burn the incense.

Burning the incense is a type of our prayer, with Christ as the incense offered to God, and lighting the lamps is a type of our dealing with the Word, that is, our reading of the Bible. Here we have a principle. Whenever we light the lamps, we have to burn the incense. That is, whenever we deal with the word in a proper way to receive light, we have to pray and offer incense to God. It is only by this kind of prayer that the word we read and understand can be transferred into the Spirit and become life to us.

Many of us read the Bible, but I am concerned that we may not read the Bible in this living way. I would recommend to you this living way. From now on, we should read the word in this way and help others to contact the Lord day by day by reading in such a way. This will cause a change among us.

PRACTICING AND DEVELOPING OUR PRAYER
WITH THE WORD TO FEAST ON THE LORD

John 14:1 through 3 says, "Do not let your heart be troubled; believe into God, believe also into Me. In My Father's house are many abodes; if it were not so, I would have told you; for I go to prepare a place for you. And if I go and prepare a place for you, I am coming again and will receive you to Myself, so that where I am you also may be." This is a good portion of the word to pray with. To pray over this portion requires a certain amount of practice, development, and consideration. We should not go too fast here. We need to taste this portion by "chewing" it. We may say, "Lord, I thank You that You went to pave the way, prepare a place, and gain the ground that I may be in the Father, that I may be in the place where You are. Lord, I do realize that today I am in the place where You are, yet I need more realization of this. Grant me more and more to experience that I am in the Father, just as You are." We should learn to apply such a portion by saying, "Lord, today keep me in the place where You are. Now I am going to my office. Keep me in the Father. Grant me the sense that I am with You in the Father all the time." When we take the word in this way, it is not merely words in black and white letters. Rather, it is living. It is in this way that we exercise our spirit and have a fresh contact with the Lord. In this way it is easy to use our spirit to pray.

As we practice to take the word in this way, we should learn to pray not merely from our knowledge but by exercising our spirit to say something from within to the Lord, to have a real contact with the Lord. We need to exercise the spirit to bring ourselves into the presence of the Lord and speak something in His presence directly, face to face. This is real prayer, not merely a prayer for affairs, business, or burdens, but a prayer to contact and digest the Lord. This is the way to feed on the Lord through the word. At the same time, while we are praying, we are drinking of the Lord.

John 5 begins, "After these things there was a feast of the Jews, and Jesus went up to Jerusalem. Now there is in Jerusalem near the sheepgate a pool, which is called in Hebrew Bethesda, having five porticoes." (vv. 1-2). This chapter is a good piece of "meat" and needs an adequate development. Since this portion is so rich, we may speak with the Lord ten, twenty, or even thirty minutes in prayer. We may say, "Lord, in that day there was a feast. I thank You that today God is my feast. In Jerusalem there was a pool with five porches. Today You are my Jerusalem, and You are my pool. There is no need for me to lie in the porches. Now I am in You; I am in Christ. There is no need for me to wait like an impotent man for the angel. You are the Angel, who has come to the place where I am. You are also the water. There is no need for me to wait for the stirring of the water. You are stirring all the time. Lord, praise You; whenever You stir, I am cured. You are also the real Sabbath to me. Lord, I praise You that today with You I have a Sabbath, a feast, a pool, an angel, the water, and the stirring."

Following this, we can apply this portion, praying, "Lord, cause me to realize all this. There is no need for me to go to heaven. You came here already, and now You are with me. You do not require or demand anything. You only supply and impart. There is no need for me to do anything or change anything. You simply impart something to me in the place where I am." If we read and pray in this way, the Bible will be a different book. It will be a living book.

We should not let a passage of the word like this go by too quickly. Perhaps the next morning we can come back to the same portion. Then we will have something more. We may pray, "Lord, I ask not only for myself but for many poor ones." We will have the burden to care for others, and we will have some genuine intercession for others. This is the living way to read the word. We all need to do this. Just as we need a meal to live physically, we also need a meal to live spiritually. We need to feed and to feast, to take something of the Lord into our spirit.

NOT BRINGING OUR RELIGIOUS CONCEPTS BUT HAVING A VISION FOR OUR PRAYER

Our prayer with the word must not be formal. When we are formal, we become religious. Often we confuse being formal and religious with being spiritual. The more we practice the living way to read the word, the more we will be genuinely spiritual and the less we will be formal and religious. If we practice this way for only half a year, we will be able to open to the same chapters and verses we read today but speak to the Lord in a different way. This will prove that we are more in the spirit and not as religious as we used to be.

It may be hard for some to know the difference between being religious and being genuinely spiritual in digesting, realizing, and applying a passage of the word. To be religious means that we know what pleases God and that we expect to be that or do that. We may pray, "Lord, help me to do that." Nearly all Christians who read Luke 21:1 to 4, for example, spontaneously ask the Lord to help them to be like the impoverished widow who cast her two coins into the treasury. On the one hand, there is nothing wrong with such a prayer, but on the other hand, it is a religious prayer.

There is no need to have a vision from the Lord to have this kind of religious concept. Even the worldly people who do not know Christ and are against Christ, when they read this portion will say, "This widow is right. If I would be a Christian, I would be like this widow." However, those worldly people have no vision. If we have the proper vision from the word, we will see that it is not a matter of offering more or less; it is a matter of doing something in the presence of the Lord. The proper vision relates to the presence of the Lord, not to being like the widow. We should pray, "Lord, help me to be in Your presence. Whatever I do, I would do it in Your presence." Whatever we do in the presence of the Lord is right.

What matters is that we live, walk, and do things in the presence of the Lord. "Lord, grant me the mercy that I may always walk and live in the sense of Your presence."

To understand this small portion of the word in a way that is not natural and religious requires a vision. When we come to the word, we must not try to understand it in a natural way. If we come to understand the word in a religious way, we need not read the word at all, because we already have a religious concept. To try to please God by offering more "coins" with greater sincerity does not require the word of God. We already had this thought in our mind even before we were saved. We should not bring religious concepts like this to the word. We need to forget them. To exercise our spirit and deny our self includes dropping all our natural and religious concepts when we come to the word.

We must come to the word without any natural understanding. Sometimes when a certain understanding comes to us, we have to check, "Is this the natural concept? Is this a religious concept?" If we practice in this way, we will learn to have discernment. Then when we come to a passage like Luke 21, we will see the vision of the presence of the Lord, and we will pray, "Lord, in whatever I do, grant me the mercy and grace that I would do it in the sense of Your presence. I would do it at Your feet. I would do it under Your watching. Whatever I do must be approved by Your presence."

Through these messages we have become clear about the proper way to read and pray. However, we all need more practice.

CHAPTER SEVEN

ENJOYING CHRIST THROUGH PRAYER

Scripture Reading: Rev. 5:8; 8:3-4; Rom. 8:26; Psa. 27:4, 8

Revelation 5:8 says, "And when He took the scroll, the four living creatures and the twenty-four elders fell before the Lamb, each having a harp and golden bowls full of incense, which bowls are the prayers of the saints." The bowls are the prayers of the saints, and within the bowls is the incense. This means that something as the incense, so sweet to God, is in the prayers of the saints. The prayer of the saints is the container, and the incense is the content.

Revelation 8:3 and 4 say, "And another Angel came and stood at the altar, having a golden censer, and much incense was given to Him to offer with the prayers of all the saints upon the golden altar which was before the throne. And the smoke of the incense went up with the prayers of the saints out of the hand of the Angel before God."

Romans 8:26 says, "Moreover, in like manner the Spirit also joins in to help us in our weakness, for we do not know for what we should pray as is fitting, but the Spirit Himself intercedes for us with groanings which cannot be uttered." Even though we know not for what we should pray, the Spirit intercedes within us and for us, many times with unutterable groanings.

Psalm 27:4 says, "One thing I have asked from Jehovah; / That do I seek: / To dwell in the house of Jehovah / All the days of my life, / To behold the beauty of Jehovah, / And to inquire in His temple." *The house of Jehovah* has two meanings. The church today is the house of God (1 Tim. 3:15), and our human spirit is also the dwelling place of the Lord (Eph. 2:22).

Psalm 27:8 says, "My heart said for thee, Seek ye my face. Thy face, O Jehovah, will I seek" (Darby's New Translation). I would also like to read this verse from the Berkeley Version: "In Thy behalf my heart proclaims, 'Seek ye My face'; Thy face, Lord, I will seek." This shows that the psalmist's heart within him said something for the Lord. His heart said, "Seek ye My face." Within his heart there was a cry and a proclamation that he had to seek the Lord's face. Then his response was, "Thy face, Lord, I will seek."

MINGLING OUR READING OF THE WORD WITH PRAYER

In this chapter we want to have more fellowship concerning enjoying Christ in an intimate way. There are always many ways to do a certain thing, but we want to know the best way. The best way to pray is to mingle our reading of the Word with our prayer. We should read the Word to enjoy the Lord. When we come to read the Word, our mind should not take the lead. As we are reading, we will spontaneously understand something. Then we can consider what we read. After our consideration, we can transfer what we understand and consider into prayer. We should pray by exercising our spirit.

We should not exercise our mind to compose a prayer. Instead, we must learn to pray with broken sentences and phrases. When we are speaking intimately to those who are close to us, we do not compose something in a formal way, yet many of us do not pray and talk to the Lord intimately. Instead, we compose something formal. This kills our spirit and helps us to exercise our mind. We must learn to pray in a very spontaneous way with terms and phrases, but without any formal composition. We should learn to be spontaneous with the Lord. As we are praying, we are reading the Word, and as we are reading, we are praying. Our praying and reading are mingled together. This is the way to deal with the Word in order to enjoy Christ.

Christ is life and everything to us for our enjoyment. On the one hand, the Lord is the Word and is in the Word. On the other hand, the Lord is the Spirit and is in the Spirit. Also, the Word is the Spirit. John 1:1 reveals that Christ was the Word in the beginning. John 6:63 shows that the Word is the

Spirit. Ephesians 6:17 shows that the Spirit is the Word. We have the Word in our hand and the Spirit in our spirit. These are the two means for us to contact and enjoy Christ. The Christian life is not a religious life but a life of enjoying Christ all the time.

Our Christian daily walk and all the virtues of the proper Christian life come out of the enjoyment of Christ. Ephesians 5 and 6 speak of wives submitting to their husbands, husbands loving their wives, children honoring their parents, fathers caring for their children, servants faithfully serving their masters, and masters treating their servants properly. Such a proper human living comes from the infilling of Christ (Eph. 5:18), which is the enjoyment of Christ. Even the fighting of the spiritual warfare at the end of Ephesians comes out of the enjoyment of Christ.

First, we can enjoy Christ by dealing with the Word. If we are going to enjoy Christ, we must know how to deal with the Word. If we do not know how to deal with the Word in a proper way, in the way of life, we can never enjoy Christ adequately. We also have to learn how to pray. To pray is to drink of Christ as the Spirit (1 Cor. 12:13). It is also to inhale Christ, to breathe Christ (John 20:22; Lam. 3:55-56). We all have to learn how to deal with the Word and how to pray, to inhale Christ as the Spirit. In praying we work together with Christ, giving Him the ground and the opportunity to work out something through us. Thus, we may say that there are two ways to enjoy Christ. One is to read the Word; the other is to pray. We need to mingle our reading of the Word with our prayer.

ENJOYING CHRIST BY PRAYING

In order to learn how to enjoy Christ by praying, we must drop the old way of prayer. Also, we should not pray for business affairs or personal concerns. Instead, pray to praise Him, to adore Him, to thank Him, to behold His beauty, and to inhale Him. Many times we have to pray by groaning, saying, "O Lord, O Lord...." This is the best prayer. The real prayer is not out of us, so that the Lord will do something for us. The real prayer is the Spirit, who is Christ Himself, working and moving within us, that we would open to Him to breathe Him out and breathe Him in (see *Hymns*, #255). We must offer Him the free way to go out and to come in to express something of Himself.

To pray is not to take care of many things. To pray is to spiritually breathe the spiritual air, which is the Lord Himself. Day by day, even several times throughout each day, we have to learn to breathe the Lord as the spiritual air. Even while we are driving our car or cooking in the kitchen we can breathe by calling from deep within, "O Lord." This is the best prayer.

Revelation shows us that the saints' prayers are the bowls or the censer that contain Christ as the incense. In our prayer there must be Christ as the incense. We have to burn the incense daily by offering prayers with Christ ascending to God. Christ is in us and we need to have the prayer as the censer, the bowls, the container, for the indwelling Christ as the incense. If we do not pray, we have Christ within us, but we do not have Him as the incense ascending to God. Proper prayer is not for our practical needs. Proper prayer is for the expression of Christ. We pray to express Christ, that is, to give the indwelling Christ the opportunity to be the incense to ascend to God and be expressed in our prayer.

Matthew 6:31 through 33 says, "Therefore do not be anxious, saying, What shall we eat? or, What shall we drink? or, With what shall we be clothed? For all these things the Gentiles are anxiously seeking. For your heavenly Father knows that you need all these things. But seek first His kingdom and His righteousness, and all these things will be added to you." We can even say to the Lord, "Lord, there is no need for me to pray for so many things. Matthew 6:31 through 33 says that You already know what I need." If we are not at peace concerning our personal needs, we can remind the Lord to feed us and care for us according to His Word. We should just seek the Lord Himself, His kingdom and His righteousness. All that we need, the Lord will not only give to us but also add to us. We should learn to pray and seek the Lord Himself to behold His beauty.

Then we can go on to learn to inquire of the Lord. This means that we must learn to ask the Lord what we have to pray. Do not pray according to what you think you have to pray, but ask the Lord what He wants you to pray in your prayer. Sometimes you may have to ask, "Lord, may I now pray for a certain friend? May I now pray for the preaching of the gospel?"

A good illustration of this is seen in Genesis 18 when the Lord came with two angels to visit Abraham. The Bible tells us that Abraham was the friend of God (2 Chron. 20:7; Isa. 41:8; James 2:23). The record in Genesis 18 shows that there was an intimate friendship between Abraham and the Lord. Abraham received the Lord as a friend, a guest, and he served the Lord (vv. 1-8). The Lord and Abraham had a mutual enjoyment. The Lord then asked Abraham, "Where is Sarah your wife?" (v. 9), and He told Abraham that his wife would bear a son (v. 10). Abraham did not ask the Lord for a son in Genesis 18. Instead, he allowed the Lord to say something to him. We should not bring many things into our prayer to intrude into our fellowship with the Lord. We should behold the Lord and let Him enjoy us as we enjoy Him. We should let Him ask us something, as He asked Abraham, "Where is your wife?" Then we should let Him say something to us.

After the Lord's fellowship with Abraham, the Lord and the two angels started to leave. Verse 16 says, "And the men rose up from there, and looked down upon Sodom; and Abraham walked with them to send them away." Darby's translation says, "Abraham went with them to conduct them." This means that Abraham escorted them. This shows how Abraham treated the Lord as an intimate friend. It was as if he said, "Lord, are You leaving? I am sorry You are going, and I am not willing to leave You. Let me escort You for a certain distance." Through Abraham's escorting and conducting the Lord, the burden for intercession came out.

Verse 17 says, "And Jehovah said, Shall I hide from Abraham what I am about to do?" Verse 17 came out of Abraham's escorting and conducting in verse 16. If Abraham would have just said, "See You again, Lord," and would not have escorted the Lord for a distance, the Lord would not have had further fellowship with him. The Lord could not hide what He was going to do from His intimate friend. He had to let him know what He was about to do.

Then the Lord told Abraham that He was going to judge Sodom. Actually, at this time the Lord had a real burden for Lot, and He needed someone to pray for Lot. The Lord always needs some intercession so that He can do something for others. Through his fellowship with the Lord, Abraham came to know the Lord's intention. Because they were intimate friends, there was no need for them to mention Lot by name.

Verses 22 and 23 say, "And the men [the two angels] turned from there, and went toward Sodom, while Abraham remained standing before the Lord. And Abraham came near and said, Will you indeed destroy the righteous with the wicked?" Even though the two angels left, Abraham was not willing to leave the Lord. He stood before the Lord for more intimate fellowship. Abraham began to intercede by asking the Lord if He would destroy the righteous with the wicked. This meant that he was praying for Lot. This shows that the burden for intercession comes from our contact with the Lord. Then the Lord reveals His heart to us, we know His intention, and His intention becomes our burden, which returns to the Lord as our intercession.

The Lord's desired intention in His heart was to save Lot from Sodom, but the Lord needed someone to pray for Lot. Without someone to pray for Lot, the Lord could not act. This is the principle of incarnation. In the new creation, in the work of the Lord's grace in salvation, there is always the need of incarnation. This means that there is always the need of someone to cooperate with the Lord. Then the Lord has the ground to do something. Genesis 19:29 indicates that when the Lord destroyed Sodom, He saved Lot to answer Abraham's prayer.

After Abraham's thorough fellowship with the Lord, Genesis tells us, "And Jehovah went away, as soon as He had finished speaking with Abraham, and Abraham returned to his place" (18:33). By reading Genesis 18 we can see that Abraham spoke, but verse 33 says that as soon as the Lord had ended His speaking to Abraham, He went away. This shows us that the best prayer is not that we speak to the Lord but that the Lord speaks to us. We should let the Lord end His speaking to us. Then we can say amen to His speaking. We should ask, "When we ended our prayer and said amen, did we end our speaking or did the Lord end His speaking?" Strictly speaking, the proper prayer is the Lord speaking through the one who prays. This is why we must learn to pray to behold His beauty and to inhale Him in order to express Him. If we do not know what to pray, we can groan, saying, "O Lord, I do not know how to pray or what to pray. O Lord...." Then we will have the best prayer.

We need to practice the fellowship in this chapter. We first must learn to read and pray over the Word. We also need to pray to behold the Lord and breathe the Lord as our spiritual air. Perhaps in the morning we can take ten or fifteen minutes for reading and praying over the Word. After this we need another time, perhaps five minutes, just to pray. We should open ourselves to the Lord, look to Him, and seek His face to behold Him, adore Him, worship Him, praise Him, and thank Him. If we have some feeling within which we do not know how to express, we can groan before Him. If we practice this kind of living and intimate prayer, we will be nourished, refreshed, and strengthened by the Lord not only in the morning but also throughout the day.

We need to learn to pray in this way all the time. First Thessalonians 5:17 charges us to pray unceasingly. It is only by this way of prayer that we can unceasingly pray. To pray in this way is to breathe spiritually. No matter what we are doing, we can pray in the way of spiritual breathing. We should breathe unceasingly, no matter what we are doing. Then we will enjoy Christ continuously.

CHAPTER EIGHT

EXERCISING OUR SPIRIT
TO ENJOY THE LORD IN PRAYER

After we have spent twenty or twenty-five minutes to
enjoy the Lord by dealing with His word, we need a time
simply to pray. During this time we should not be preoccupied
with what we have read. We should keep nothing in mind and
simply seek His face, open ourselves, behold Him, look to
Him, and speak something about Him, about His goodness
and beauty, to adore and worship Him.

At first, some may begin their prayer by saying, "Lord, I
confess that I do not know how to enjoy You or praise You in
this way." This may be good, but it is only the beginning of the
practice of prayer. After we practice this kind of prayer some
more, we should not say that we do not know how. Rather,
when we come to the Lord, we should express something very
positively from our inner realization. We may realize that the
Lord is sweet, so we can pray, "O Lord, You are so sweet!" We
may also realize that the Lord is so available, so we can say,
"Lord, I adore You! You are so available. O Lord, I adore You
and praise You for Your availability." In this way we can
speak something positively with assurance and confirmation.

PRAYING TO EXPRESS
OUR INNER REALIZATION OF THE LORD

To say that we do not know how to praise the Lord is an
excuse. Eventually the Lord will not allow us this excuse. He
may say, "You do know how to praise Me." We have realized
many things concerning the Lord, so we simply should
express something in prayer from our inner realization. The
adoration, worship, praise, and thanks that we render to the

Lord are the expressions of our inner realization. We may say to a brother, for example, "O brother, you are so kind." This is a kind of praise to that brother, which is the expression of our realization about him. In the same way, within our being we realize something of the Lord. This inner realization is expressed sometimes as adoration, sometimes as praise, and sometimes as the thanks we render to the Lord. Sometimes we need to say, "O Lord, I love Your presence. I love to behold Your beauty. I am here to open to You. O Lord, open Yourself more to me."

We are at the beginning of this kind of practice. After a certain period of practice, we will get away from compositions and explanations in our prayer. The more we practice to pray in this way, the more we will be simple in our expressions. The basic principle is simply to express our inner realization of the Lord.

A brother may pray, "Lord, You have made it clear to me that You live and dwell in my spirit." This kind of prayer may merely be a kind of explanation or definition. Instead, we should express something of our inner realization. We may say, "O Lord, what a grace! What a grace, Lord, that You are here. What a grace that You are with me, and what a grace that You are in my spirit! O Lord, so sweet!" This is the expression of the realization that the Lord lives in us.

In the first one or two weeks of our practice to pray in this way, we may define and compose our words very neatly. After a certain period of practice, however, we will be more simple. Our prayers will be expressions, not definitions or explanations. Our prayers may simply be short sentences or even simple phrases. We may say, "O Lord, how good that You are with me all the time." In this way we can forget about our natural mind and exercise our spirit. When we pray, we have to concentrate all our strength in our spirit to speak something: "O Lord, what a mercy! What a grace! Oh, how good it is! O Lord! Hallelujah! I just cannot express it. It is too good." This is to say something from the spirit, not to compose a prayer. If we pray with broken sentences and do not compose our prayers, we will have the release of the spirit. Our spirit will be released and uplifted. Please try this.

This is the way even to speak a message. When a young brother first begins to minister, he often prepares an introduction and each part of the message in a proper composition. As he advances, however, he leaves this kind of formality behind and speaks to people in a more effective and releasing way.

Some may pray with too much composition because they are accustomed to praying publicly in the meetings. However, even when praying in the meetings, we should learn to express rather than to explain. Rather than praying in an explaining way, "Lord, it is a privilege for us to be before You at this time," we may simply express, "O Lord, what a precious time! How precious that we can be here." This is an expression, not an explanation. Our present way of prayer proves that in the past we have become accustomed to an old way. Now we must practice to pray in a new way, with short and even broken sentences. Our explanations and definitions must become expressions of our inner realization. We should not care about thinking, considerations, and compositions. We simply should take care of our inner realization.

PRAYING NOT WITH COMPOSED UTTERANCES BUT WITH THE RICHES OF CHRIST

If we see a building on fire, we would not say to our neighbor, "My dear friend, you must know that there is a fire close by." No one would compose in such a way. Rather, we would cry, "Fire!" This is an expression, not an explanation. We must learn to pray in the way of expressing something from our inner realization. Within ourselves we realize something of the Lord, so we simply express it. Many of the Psalms in the Old Testament are spoken in this way. They do not explain things; rather, they express something. How much more should this be the case with us today. Too many of us have learned the wrong way to pray. That is the religious, natural way. We have to change our way. If the dear brothers among us would take this word to practice to pray from our inner realization, our prayer will be much improved.

The more we practice, the more we will be delivered from the way of composition. If we reduce our composing, we will have more expression, and when we have more expression, we will have the riches not of composition but of the items of the Lord. We may say, "O Lord, You are my food, my drink, and my breath. Oh, my fresh air! My strength and my enlightening." The Lord as food, drink, and breath are His riches. Then we will continue, "You are my satisfaction. Oh, the preciousness and freshness of this air! O Lord, how refreshing! It is beyond words to express." This kind of prayer is rich in essence, not in composition, sentences, clauses, and words. The more we pray in this way, the more we will absorb the Lord.

We need to practice this kind of prayer again and again. We must learn not to compose but to express something from within our spirit to contact the Lord with simple utterances, the shorter the better. If we do this, we will sense the riches of Christ, and we will have the application and practicality of the experience of Christ in our daily walk. We enjoy Him all the time, so when we come to Him, we have a certain realization, a certain sense. We may have enjoyed the Lord much throughout the whole afternoon. Then in the evening we may have five minutes to pray before dinner. There is no need to close our door or even to kneel down. Wherever we are, we can simply express something to the Lord: "O Lord, what a strengthening throughout my whole afternoon! I adore You, Lord. You are my strength." The more we pray in this way, the more we will be strengthened, the more we will enjoy Him, and the more we will absorb Him.

NOT CARING FOR OUR NATURAL MIND BUT EXERCISING OUR SPIRIT TO PRAY

The Psalms were written in the way of expressions to the Lord. However, so many New Testament Christians cannot compare with the Old Testament psalmists. They have the indwelling Spirit, but they do not use their spirit to pray with simple expressions. It is not that we should pray with Old Testament terms, such as, "So panteth my soul after thee, O God" (Psa. 42:1 KJV). Rather, it is that the principle of the psalmists is right: "O God, my soul pants for You!" We all must learn to change our way of praying. I believe that if we do this, the brothers and sisters will be more living, and the meetings will also be more living.

Even if we pray with a good spirit, we may still have too much composition in our prayer. This is because we all "graduated from the same school" where we majored in the same field of old prayers. We need to drop the composition in our prayers. We must learn to pray by exercising our spirit to express something, not by exercising our mind to compose something. This is the proper principle of prayer. Any muscle we use is always strengthened and enlarged. It is the same with our spirit. The more we use our spirit, the more it will be enlarged and strengthened.

In prayer we must learn to concentrate our spirit and forget our natural mind. We should not compose anything but simply express something from within according to our realization and sense. We need to have an inward sense of the Lord. We can sense Him not only as our food, our drink, and our portion but as many other items. Sometimes we may say, "O Lord, I am experiencing Your sovereignty. Throughout this whole day, what sovereignty I have experienced." This is the expression of our experience of the Lord at that time. We all have to learn this way. Then I believe our meetings will be very enriched by our prayers of this kind.

After a certain amount of practice, we will change the way of our prayer. We will spontaneously say, "Lord, Your presence is precious, so sweet!" If we sense that we are in the mind, we should not explain this to the Lord, saying, "In the past I have been too much in the mind. How much I am in the mind. Help me to realize that I have to exercise my spirit. But Lord, I do not know how to do this." This is a good prayer, but it is too much in the mind with composing, explaining, and reasoning. If we were in an earthquake, there would be no time to explain anything. We would just cry, "Earthquake!" In the same way, we can simply cry, "Lord, deliver me from the mind. O Lord, from the mind! Deliver me! What a mercy, Lord! What a grace! You are here in my spirit. O Lord, help me to exercise my spirit. Oh, the spirit! Lord, the spirit! O Lord, help me to exercise!" This is real prayer. It is an expression, not an explanation. After praying in this way for five minutes, we will be in the heavens. Go to practice this. You will see the difference. Your prayer will be absolutely different.

PRAYING SHORT PRAYERS WITH A STRONG SPIRIT IN THE MEETINGS

To pray in the way of composing, we do not need any boldness. We may be weak in our spirit and self-conscious. To pray in the way of expressing our realization, however, requires boldness, strength in the spirit, and deliverance from self-consciousness. The stronger our spirit is, the shorter the sentences and clauses of our prayer will be. The more living our prayer is, the shorter the wording will be and the less natural reasoning there will be in our utterance. We must learn to pray in this new way. Then when we come to the meeting, we can pray in the same way, in the way not of explaining but of expressing. Learn to pray in this way.

I say again, we need more practice. We should practice this way of prayer not only in our private times but in the meetings. Of course, the need in the meeting will not always be the same. Sometimes we need a long prayer like Psalm 119, the longest psalm, with one hundred seventy-six verses in twenty-two stanzas of eight verses each. However, most of the time our prayer in the meetings should be living, strong, and short to express something of our realization of the Lord. Short prayers that are not wordy are richer in their effect. To speak a wordy prayer means that we are praying in the mind. When we pray in the spirit, our words are cut short. We need to practice these two matters: to contact the Lord by dealing with the word, and to pray in this new way to enjoy Him.

CHAPTER NINE

PRAYING TO ENJOY THE LORD
AND EXPRESS HIS BURDEN

Scripture Reading: Eph. 5:18-20; 6:18-20; Jude 20; Gen. 18:16-33; 1 Sam. 1:10-11; Luke 1:46-55

In this message we will consider the proper way to enjoy the Lord, partake of Him, and intercede by expressing His burden in prayer.

PRAYER BEING THE ISSUE
OF OUR ENJOYMENT OF THE LORD

Ephesians 3:16 and 17a say, "That He would grant you, according to the riches of His glory, to be strengthened with power through His Spirit into the inner man, that Christ may make His home in your hearts through faith." Verse 19b says, "That you may be filled unto all the fullness of God." Following this, 5:18 through 20 tell us what kind of persons are strengthened by the Spirit into the inner man, occupied in their heart by Christ, and are filled in their entire being unto all the fullness of God. These verses say, "And do not be drunk with wine, in which is dissoluteness, but be filled in spirit, speaking to one another in psalms and hymns and spiritual songs, singing and psalming with your heart to the Lord, giving thanks at all times for all things in the name of our Lord Jesus Christ to our God and Father."

Psalms, hymns, praises, and thanks are the overflow of being filled in spirit. The fact that this overflow includes singing indicates that it is an enjoyment. Whenever we sing, that is a strong proof that we are enjoying something. Therefore, to be filled in spirit is to enjoy the Lord, and in such a condition we pour out praises and thanks to God. Praises and thanks are the overflow of the inner enjoyment of Christ. Moreover, it is from this enjoyment that the proper living of husbands, wives, children, parents, servants, and masters issue forth in the Christian life (vv. 22, 25; 6:1, 4, 5, 9).

After this, Ephesians tells us that we are entitled and burdened to fight the battle to deal with the enemy of God (6:10-20). In this way, this book concludes with prayer. Verses 18 through 20 say, "By means of all prayer and petition, praying at every time in spirit and watching unto this in all perseverance and petition concerning all the saints, and for me, that utterance may be given to me in the opening of my mouth, to make known in boldness the mystery of the gospel, for which I am an ambassador in a chain, that in it I would speak boldly, as I ought to speak." When we are filled with the Lord and enjoy Him, we have all the proper items of the Christian life as an issue of this enjoyment. Then we are enabled, entitled, and burdened to fight the battle to deal with God's enemy by praying always in the spirit with all prayer and petition.

BEING FILLED WITH THE SPIRIT
TO PRAY IN THE HOLY SPIRIT

Jude 20 says, "But you, beloved, building up yourselves upon your most holy faith, praying in the Holy Spirit." In order to pray in the Holy Spirit, we must be filled with Him; we must inhale Him into us.

A MARVELOUS EXAMPLE OF INTERCESSION

Genesis 18 contains a good illustration and a great help concerning prayer. This chapter records a conversation and a conference between Abraham and the Lord. The Lord came to Abraham with two of His angels. Abraham received the Lord, served Him, and ministered to Him, and the Lord enjoyed what Abraham ministered (vv. 1-8). Then while the Lord was enjoying that, He told Abraham what He would do for his wife Sarah, in that she would bring forth a son (v. 10). It seems that this contact between the Lord and Abraham was sufficient.

However, when the Lord and the two angels began to leave,

Abraham was not willing to lose His presence, so he escorted them for a certain distance. Verses 16 through 24 say, "And the men rose up from there and looked down upon Sodom; and Abraham walked with them to send them away. And Jehovah said, Shall I hide from Abraham what I am about to do, since Abraham will indeed become a great and mighty nation, and all the nations of the earth will be blessed in him? For I know him, that he will command his children and his household after him to keep the way of Jehovah by doing righteousness and justice, that Jehovah may bring upon Abraham what He has spoken concerning him. And Jehovah said, The cry of Sodom and Gomorrah, how great it is; and their sin, how very heavy it is! I shall go down and see whether they have done altogether according to its outcry, which has come to Me; and if not, I will know. And the men turned from there and went toward Sodom, while Abraham remained standing before Jehovah. And Abraham came near and said, Will You indeed destroy the righteous with the wicked? Suppose there are fifty righteous within the city; will You indeed destroy and not spare the place for the sake of the fifty righteous who are in it?"

Verses 32 and 33 conclude this portion, saying, "And he said, Oh let the Lord not be angry if I speak yet once more. Suppose ten are found there? And He said, I will not destroy it because of ten. And Jehovah went away as soon as He had finished speaking with Abraham, and Abraham returned to his place."

It was when Abraham was unwilling to lose the Lord's presence that the Lord said, "Shall I hide from Abraham what I am about to do?" This is the imparting of the Lord's burden for intercession. Within the heart of the Lord there was a burden, and at this time the Lord found the right person to share this burden with. Suppose, however, that when the Lord began to leave, Abraham simply said good-bye. That would have been the end of their contact, and no burden for intercession would have been revealed to Abraham.

Within the Lord there was a very tender feeling. He did not impart His burden to Abraham before he conducted Him for a certain distance. Rather, the Lord kept His burden hidden. It was not until Abraham escorted Him that He imparted His burden. Then it was as if He said, "How can I hide from Abraham what I am about to do? I have to let him know."

At that time, the Lord revealed to Abraham His strong concern for Sodom. In actuality, His concern was for Lot, who was in Sodom. In this way Abraham came to know what was in the Lord's heart, so Abraham was burdened to intercede for Lot. Abraham prayed in a personal way, in a way of consulting with the Lord and making a bargain with Him. The Lord agreed that if there were fifty righteous souls, He would spare Sodom, but since Abraham realized there were not fifty, he reduced the number to forty-five, forty, thirty, twenty, and ten. This intercession was a kind of conference and consultation between Abraham and the Lord.

Apparently Abraham spoke much with the Lord. However, at the end of this account verse 33 says, "And Jehovah went away as soon as He had finished speaking with Abraham, and Abraham returned to his place." It does not say that when Abraham ended his speaking with the Lord, he said amen and left. Instead, it says that the Lord ended His speaking and left. This is a good illustration of proper intercession.

PRAYING BY CONFESSING
AND ABSORBING THE LORD INTO US

The proper prayer is a prayer in which we enjoy the Lord, drinking and inhaling Him into us. This is the first thing we should do when we come to pray. If anything frustrates us from praying in this way, we must realize that there is something wrong between us and the Lord and deal with it by confessing. We should say, "Lord, there must be something wrong with me. Reveal to me what is wrong." If we are open to the Lord, the Holy Spirit will give us the sense that we are wrong in certain things, and we should follow that sense to confess our wrongdoings and apply the Lord's blood. If after this we still have the sense that something is frustrating us, yet we do not know what it is, we should ask the Lord to cover us and cleanse us concerning whatever it is with His precious blood. We can take the standing of the cleansing of His blood, claiming it by faith. Then right away we should forget about the frustrating sense, look to the Lord, and absorb something of Him. We need to learn to enjoy the Lord in this way.

We need to spend a certain amount of time to absorb the Lord. We cannot do it in a fast way. We should look to the Lord and speak something about the Lord Himself. This is to breathe Him in. We should not first pray for many things according to our memory. When we come to the Lord, we need to forget about those things and not be burdened for anything other than the Lord Himself. We simply must come to contact Him, breathe Him in, and enjoy Him. This is the first matter in prayer.

PRAYING TO EXPRESS THE LORD'S HEART AFTER WE ARE FILLED WITH HIM

The second main item of prayer is to express something of the Lord. This means that the Lord must burden us with some desire of His heart. His heart's desire becomes a burden to us. After we have inhaled the Lord and absorbed something of Him into us, what we have absorbed becomes a burden within us, and we express this burden in prayer. This is the genuine and proper way to pray.

Sometimes this expression in prayer may be concerning our condition. The Lord may burden us that we are fleshly or sloppy. If He does this, we should have nothing different to say. Whatever else we say will not have the anointing. We may have the anointing only to say, "Lord, deliver me from my present situation. I am so fleshly, and I am so sloppy. Grant me full deliverance." Sometimes we have to cry out and even weep with tears in our prayer. The more we pray in this way, the more we will touch and be touched by the anointing.

After we hear a message exhorting us not to be fleshly and sloppy, we may go to the Lord in our own effort and pray about our fleshiness and sloppiness. However, this does not work, and it brings out no change within us. We should not try to correct ourselves in this way. Rather, we must first go to the Lord to deal with every frustrating and negative thing, and then we must absorb the Lord, enjoy Him, and take Him in. Then something of the Lord Himself within us will burden us to pray.

Sometimes the Lord's burden will be something for the church, for a certain brother, or for a certain work. That is the right time to pray for the church, to pray for that brother, or to pray for that work. This is not a prayer initiated by ourselves. It is a prayer initiated by the Lord within. This is more than just a petition to the Lord; it is an expression of the Lord. We express the Lord from within because we have been filled with the Lord. Our prayer is something of the Lord, even the Lord Himself, for us to express. This is the proper way to pray, not only to enjoy the Lord but also to express the Lord through intercession. To pray in this way is to pray in the Holy Spirit. We have received something of the Lord, and we are filled with Him within. Now because we have inhaled and absorbed the Lord, whatever we pray will be something from the Holy Spirit.

Many Christians practice to pray according to a prayer list or notebook of names. When they go to pray, they first check the proper entry in their prayer notebook. These, of course, are very good and devoted Christians, and sometimes the Lord works sovereignly through this kind of prayer. The Lord is gracious. Like the air, He comes into any place where there is even a small crack. However, this does not mean that this way of prayer is the right way. It is not the best way. The best way to pray can be compared to opening the windows. The brothers who take care of the meeting hall come before the meeting to open the windows and the doors. This is the right way to let the air in. If there is a hole in the glass or a crack in a board, the air can force itself in, but that is a poor way to let the air in. Similarly, the best way to pray is to "open our windows" to heaven, that is, to open ourselves to the Lord and contact Him. We all must learn day by day to open ourselves to the Lord, to "open our windows" to Him, just like Daniel prayed toward Jerusalem through his open windows three times a day (Dan. 6:10).

We need to open ourselves to the Lord and spend time with Him. We must not think that we do not have enough time. We should make no excuses about our time. The sisters are busy with cooking, washing, and many things, but they cannot say that they have no time to breathe. Even while they are cooking, they must open themselves to the Lord. In the past year and a half, we have composed two hundred thirty new hymns. Many times while I was composing, I said, "Lord, I open to You. O Lord, come in." This illustrates that we cannot say that we are too busy to pray. While we are working, we need to open ourselves to the Lord. To pray in a closed room may be necessary sometimes, but this is not the normal, healthy way. Once when I had an illness for two and a half years, I spent much time to breathe in a concerted way. However, that was an abnormal situation. Today when I am healthy, I breathe all the time, whatever I do, wherever I go, and with whomever I contact.

We have to learn to contact the Lord in this way. We must open ourselves to the Lord to absorb something of Him into us. If we sense a frustration, we should immediately ask the Lord what is wrong and confess it. If we are not clear about what specifically is wrong, we should tell the Lord that we are under His blood, and we apply its cleansing. Then we have to contact the Lord by faith to praise Him, look to Him, appreciate Him, adore Him, behold His beauty, and stay in His presence for a certain time to praise Him and speak something concerning Him.

The more we contact the Lord in this way, the more we are filled with Him. After we enjoy the Lord, there will spontaneously be a deep sense within us, and we will have a burden to pray. We will forget our own affairs, problems, burdens, and troubles, and gradually we will have the burden of intercession. We will have the burden in prayer to express something of the Lord, and we can inquire of the Lord whether or not that is His burden, just as Abraham became burdened with the Lord's desire concerning Lot and prayed while conversing and consulting with the Lord. After inhaling the Lord and being filled with Him, we will have the burden to pray, sometimes for ourselves and sometimes for our family, the church, the saints, the gospel, sinners, and even for the churches in faraway places. We will be one with the Lord to enjoy Him and express Him. This is the proper meaning of praying in the

Holy Spirit. It is only in this way that we can pray in the Holy Spirit and pray unceasingly (1 Thes. 5:17).

There is no need to be formal or to have a good composition in our prayers. Instead, we should speak freely with the Lord. The more we practice to pray in this way, the more we will pray in simple words, even in single words. Many times we may simply sigh in our prayer. These sighs are like the "selah" in the Psalms or like the rests in musical notations. This makes our prayer more meaningful. After praying for a while, we can pause for refreshment and a rest, a selah. We should not rush or utter something too quickly. Our resting gives the Lord a chance to utter something. If we have a small silence in our speaking, the Lord will give us further utterance. Sometimes we need to rest and even grope for utterance. This will give the Lord a chance to impress us with some new utterance. It is easy to practice our personal times of prayer in this way.

AVOIDING NATURAL AND RELIGIOUS CONCEPTS IN OUR PRAYER

When we pray to adore the Lord and praise Him, we have to learn to drop the natural and religious thought. We have many positive items from the Scriptures with which we can praise the Lord. There is no need for us to use utterance that comes from the religious, natural feeling. We should learn to speak things from deep within and also to use the utterances from the Bible. We see this kind of speaking in the prayer of Samuel's mother (1 Sam. 1:10-11) and the praise of Mary, the mother of the Lord Jesus (Luke 1:46-55). We also need to learn to pray in the way Paul prayed in Ephesians 1:17 through 23 and 3:14 through 21. When we praise and adore the Lord, we need to drop our natural thought, concept, and feeling and speak something heavenly, spiritual, new, full of life, full of the anointing, and full of the sweetness of the Lord.

Whenever we come to pray, we must not bring our old things to the Lord. We simply must come to contact the Lord and open ourselves to Him. We should not consider what to say. We should forget our natural mentality and learn to sense something of the Lord within, exercising the inner sense to speak something to Him. We need not compose our utterance. Rather, when we sense something in our spirit, in the depths of our being, we should express it in a brief way. To compose our prayer will frustrate the inner sense. If, for example, we sense that the Lord is sweet, we can say, "O Lord! Oh, You are so sweet." The Lord knows what we mean; there is no need to complete our utterance. Sometimes according to our sense we may pray, "O Lord, You are so deep. This satisfies me." It is sufficient simply to utter something from within us with simple words and phrases, without any composition. We should simply express our inner sense.

For this purpose, we need to spend adequate time in our prayer. If possible, we should shut ourselves up with the Lord and not let anything intrude into our time with Him. Then we will have something to express. If we do not have something to express, we should not compose anything. There is no such law that every time we enjoy the Lord we must have a burden to express. To do this may be of our own manufacture. If we do not have something particular to express, we should just enjoy the Lord. It may be that in the morning we simply enjoy Him, and then two hours later the expression will come. At that time we may spontaneously have a burden to pray. This will be something with which the Lord burdens us. We must not make our coming to the Lord into a routine. This will deaden us. Instead, the principle is this—we come to the Lord to open ourselves and to sense a burden to pray.

THE BURDEN OF OUR PRAYER
HAVING ONE MAIN FOCUS

When we come into the presence of the Lord to pray with a burden, we need to focus on one matter at a time. We cannot come to a feast to eat too many dishes at once. To pray for many different matters without focusing on a real burden may indicate that our practice is merely religious. When we pray in this way, we cannot tell in particular for what we have prayed. When we come to the Lord, we should be touched by Him with a certain matter. Sometimes we may be touched by the love of the Lord, His holiness, or His presence. When we receive a certain matter from the Lord, we will be burdened for that one thing.

Consider Daniel's prayer in Daniel 9:3 through 19. It was a long prayer, but it stressed mainly one point—the revelation that at the expiration of seventy years the Lord would release His people and bring them back from captivity (v. 2). Daniel was burdened for what he saw, and his prayer concentrated on that one matter. Similarly, Psalm 119 with one hundred seventy-six verses is the longest chapter in the Scriptures, but it focuses on only one thing—the word of God. There is a real burden in the praise of that Psalm. Our prayer should have one main focus. It is difficult to have two burdens at one time. We cannot tell if such a prayer is "beef, mutton, or pork." If our prayer is a collection of many items together without a real burden, that may indicate that it is out of our natural self and religious knowledge.

We need to drop the things from our natural and religious background and come to the Lord with a single, simple heart and an open spirit to be touched by Him. If we learn not to speak naturally, we will speak in a proper way. A young musician once applied to learn under an expert in Italy. That expert said to him, "I will receive you as a student on one condition. For three years you must not open your mouth to speak." The young man considered whether or not he could learn anything if he did not speak, but eventually he agreed to the condition. He remained under that tutor for three years until one day the tutor told him, "Now speak to express your feeling." Once the young man began to speak, what he expressed was everything that the tutor had taught him. If the student had been allowed to express himself for those three years, that would have been a frustration to his learning. In the same way, many times we need to come to the Lord to be silent. At such times we should say nothing from ourselves but let the Lord teach us what to say.

We must avoid all religious thought and understanding when we pray. Sometimes we have to pray with a long prayer, but still we need to concentrate on a main burden. Sometimes we may pray, "Lord, be merciful to me." That is a good prayer. In Matthew 20:32 and 33 Jesus asked two blind men, "What do you want Me to do for you?" They replied, "Lord, that our eyes may be opened." As a prayer, that was good enough. There was no need to say, "Lord, I know You are the Son of David. You came with the power of God. You are sovereign. You can do everything. If You will, You can heal me." We should learn not to speak in this way when we pray. Then we will have something proper to speak. The more we pray, the more we enjoy the Lord, absorb Him, and inhale Him. Then we will have a burden that comes out of our being filled with the Lord, and we can utter and express something of the Lord.

ABOUT THE AUTHOR

Witness Lee was born in 1905 in northern China and raised in a Christian family. At age 19 he was fully captured for Christ and immediately consecrated himself to preach the gospel for the rest of his life. Early in his service, he met Watchman Nee, a renowned preacher, teacher, and writer. Witness Lee labored together with Watchman Nee under his direction. In 1934 Watchman Nee entrusted Witness Lee with the responsibility for his publication operation, called the Shanghai Gospel Bookroom.

Prior to the Communist takeover in 1949, Witness Lee was sent by Watchman Nee and his other co-workers to Taiwan to insure that the things delivered to them by the Lord would not be lost. Watchman Nee instructed Witness Lee to continue the former's publishing operation abroad as the Taiwan Gospel Bookroom, which has been publicly recognized as the publisher of Watchman Nee's works outside China. Witness Lee's work in Taiwan manifested the Lord's abundant blessing. From a mere 350 believers, newly fled from the mainland, the churches in Taiwan grew to 20,000 in five years.

In 1962 Witness Lee felt led of the Lord to come to the United States, settling in California. During his 35 years of service in the U.S., he ministered in weekly meetings and weekend conferences, delivering several thousand spoken messages. Much of his speaking has since been published as over 400 titles. Many of these have been translated into over fourteen languages. He gave his last public conference in February 1997 at the age of 91.

He leaves behind a prolific presentation of the truth in the Bible. His major work, *Life-study of the Bible,* comprises over 25,000 pages of commentary on every book of the Bible from the perspective of the believers' enjoyment and experience of God's divine life in Christ through the Holy Spirit. Witness Lee was the chief editor of a new translation of the New Testament into Chinese called the Recovery Version and directed the translation of the same into English. The Recovery Version also appears in a number of other languages. He provided an extensive body of footnotes, outlines, and spiritual cross references. A radio broadcast of his messages can be heard on Christian radio stations in the United States. In 1965 Witness Lee founded Living Stream Ministry, a non-profit corporation, located in Anaheim, California, which officially presents his and Watchman Nee's ministry.

Witness Lee's ministry emphasizes the experience of Christ as life and the practical oneness of the believers as the Body of Christ. Stressing the importance of attending to both these matters, he led the churches under his care to grow in Christian life and function. He was unbending in his conviction that God's goal is not narrow sectarianism but the Body of Christ. In time, believers began to meet simply as the church in their localities in response to this conviction. In recent years a number of new churches have been raised up in Russia and in many eastern European countries.

OTHER BOOKS PUBLISHED BY
Living Stream Ministry

Titles by Witness Lee:

Titles by Watchman Nee:

Available at
Christian bookstores, or contact Living Stream Ministry
2431 W. La Palma Ave. • Anaheim, CA 92801
1-800-549-5164 • www.livingstream.com